Revie

Can't put it down. Brava."

-Rosanna Arquette

"I've started reading the last one. You've got talent my friend."

-Virginia Giuffre

"It is wonderful – highly original and a wonderful sprint through the glamorous global big business and high society."

-Alexis Parr, journalist for *The DailyMail*

"What they don't understand is that Kirby Sommers is Batman. Watching her work, marveling at what she has accomplished, it is impossible not to admire her."

-Greg Olear

Books by Kirby Sommers

Non-Fiction

New! Chasing Chandler
New! Creating Epstein: Bill Barr, Leslie
Wexner & the CIA
New! Epstein's Women
Jeffrey Epstein Predator Spy
Ghislaine Maxwell: An Unauthorized
Biography
Jeffrey Epstein, Revealed (co-written with
Bob Fitrakis)
Bonnie's Clyde: The True Story of Jeffrey
Epstein & Ghislaine Maxwell

Ask Me Anything: About Jeffrey Epstein &
Ghislaine Maxwell (with Bob Fitrakis)
Best of Epstein Project
Epstein Project: Book One
Epstein Project: Book Two
Jeffrey Epstein & El Chapo
Franklin Scandal & Presidio Child Abuse
Power, Money, Politics & Sex

Memoir

The Billionaire's Woman: A Memoir
Cinderella Doesn't Live Here Anymore
Love in the Time of Sickness

Renting in New York

Guerrilla Guide to Renting in NYC
Landlord Links Series

Upcoming Books

Ghislaine Maxwell, Blackmail
Cinderella Doesn't Live Here Anymore

For previews of upcoming books and members only events, please add yourself to Kirby Sommers' mailing list. It is on her website:

kirbysommers.com/mailing-list

Kirby is also on Twitter @kirbysommers

GHISLAINE MAXWELL

An Unauthorized Biography

Ghislaine Maxwell: An Unauthorized Biography

GHISLAINE MAXWELL

An Unauthorized Biography

Kirby Sommers

Foreword by Greg Olear

Ghislaine Maxwell: An Unauthorized Biography

Copyright 2021-2022 Kirby Sommers

CONTENTS

ACKNOWLEDGEMENT

I want to thank all the people I've met during my journey as I researched the Jeffrey Epstein and Ghislaine Maxwell case. My many followers on Twitter, some of whom have become friends, and the many people who have cheered me on in ways that changed the trajectory of my life.

Thank you to my readers. To everyone who read one book and then came back for a second, then a third, and then yet another. Without you, I wouldn't be here now writing these words.

I want to thank Matthew Steeples for his unflinching ability to find the true story through the haze and clutter. He understood that I was a victim of the same machine inhabited by the likes of Jeffrey Epstein and Ghislaine Maxwell. While other journalists simply took my tweets and labeled them their own, Matthew respected my work, and credited me accordingly. It is because of this that I felt comfortable allowing him to print several of the chapters of my book in his online newspaper, *The Steeple Times*.

I want to thank Carey Fox who always made time to hear my thoughts and who had a front row seat allowing him to witness the events in my life steering me in one direction and then another. When I was a little girl I wanted to grow up to become a writer. Life had other plans for me. However, it was Carey, time and time again, who assured me I possessed the talent and indeed had a gift. For his unwavering belief in me and his encouragement I will forever be grateful.

Sometimes, when one takes a path less traveled, one is likely to meet similar minded people. I was fortunate to have met Greg Olear. Greg is a gifted writer. He is a man of enormous depth who also possesses the rare gift of seeing beyond the surface. When I asked him to write the Foreword for this book—he didn't hesitate. His willingness to help and his belief in my work encouraged me in ways he will never know.

Much gratitude and thanks to Philip Fokker, who edited this book, and who caught with his gift of clarity what my eyes missed. Without his patience this book would have taken far longer to complete.

Thank you to Bruce Lambert, former New York Times journalist and dear friend, who made it possible for me to embark on a new journey at a time when I believed no new journey was possible.

And, thank you to the victims, now survivors, of Jeffrey Epstein and Ghislaine Maxwell, whose endless courage shows us all that anything is possible.

FOREWORD

———————————

It was bound to happen sooner or later. The laws of karma demanded it. One of the victims of the unimaginably horrific global sex trafficking trade would survive the abuse, baptize herself in the fire of her torment, and rise up to take on her oppressors. That is who Kirby Sommers is, and that is what she has, against all odds, managed to do.

When Bruce Wayne was a boy, he watched helplessly as his parents were murdered by a common street thug. Most people would never have recovered from such devastating trauma. Not young Bruce. He dedicated himself to a life of crimefighting, and became the Batman.

Kirby's origin story is more horrifying than Bruce Wayne's. Impregnated by her rapist—who forced his way into her apartment after their movie date—she was desperate for money to get an abortion. For help, she turned to her older sister, who was something of a mother figure to her. It was her sister, her own flesh and blood, who introduced her to the brothel, who fed her to the cruel machine of sex trafficking. That initial betrayal led Kirby Sommers to be claimed by a man who was fabulously wealthy, but also sick, perverted, and evil—a comic book bad guy, but all too real.

For years Kirby was his sex slave—not in a *Story of O* sort of way, but an actual slave, effectively owned by this man, forced to indulge his disgusting carnal desires. When she finally escaped from his clutches, she had her Bruce Wayne moment: she dedicated her life to exposing not only him, but all of the abominable predators like him. That meant, primarily, the ne plus ultra of sex trafficking villains, Jeffrey Epstein. It was through her relentless, painstaking work on the Epstein case that I got to know Kirby's work.

The machine went on the attack, as it does. The men (it's mostly but not exclusively men) in this perverted club are men of privilege and power and wealth, and they use every means at their disposal to silence their accusers. Victims are discredited, trolled, sued, harassed, threatened, mentally abused—whatever tactics their devious minds cook up. Petty males have been doing this for centuries, to Lidia, to Catherine the Great, to any powerful woman they perceive as a threat. Kirby is no exception. To this day, her abuser wants us to think she's nuts, that her work is garbage, that she has some ulterior motive in doing what she does.

What they don't understand is that Kirby Sommers is Batman. Watching her work, marveling at what she has accomplished, it is impossible not to admire her.

Bruce Wayne had Alfred the Butler, a mansion, and millions of dollars inherited from his father to ease his transition into Batmanhood. Being neither fictional nor rich, Kirby lacks these fantastical resources. But she doesn't need them, because like the Caped Crusader, she is relentless, unwavering, and steadfast in her quest to root out the evildoers.

My privilege, being a white man, is to turn away, to stop looking, to think about other things. Kirby never looks away. She is always watching. She is forever vigilant. And she will never stop. That is her superpower.

And now, she has fixed her gaze on the vilest *female* villain since Elizabeth Báthory. In the larger story of the global sex trafficking trade, Ghislaine Maxwell is one of the most infamous, and most formidable, bad guys. Her father was a notorious spy, a foreigner who managed to ingratiate himself into the highest reaches of the British establishment. Her business partner Jeffrey Epstein was also a spy and an arms dealer, as well as a prolific sex trafficker and collector of *kompromat*. Already tight with Britain's Prince Andrew, as a New York socialite, Ghislaine Maxwell befriended the rich and powerful. Her sisters work in Big Tech. Her boyfriend—or is he her husband?—works in shipping. How does this make any sense? Who is Ghislaine Maxwell, really? And how did she become such a monster?

In this remarkable volume, Kirby Sommers finds out. She always finds out.

—PREVAIL columnist and podcaster Greg Olear (@gregolear) is the author of Dirty Rubles: An Introduction to Trump/Russia.

AUTHOR'S NOTE

Ghislaine Maxwell has been in the public eye since birth. Ninth child of disgraced media baron Robert Maxwell, who died mysteriously on November 5, 1991 with billions in debt, she was said by her father to be the one most like him.

In this book, I trace her life from birth to when she begins to collaborate with Jeffrey Epstein after the death of her father.

While there were photographs and articles of Ghislaine that served me well in connecting the pieces of her life, I discovered as I progressed, these same photos and articles were scrubbed from the internet. It seemed fairly obvious that someone or some *entity* wanted her early life to vanish from the inquisitive eyes of the public. For a woman who lived life as a socialite, it was curious to watch her disappear before my eyes.

This is somewhat similar to what her father did whenever journalists began poking around in his private and public matters. While he lived his debauched life in the era before the internet, he took other steps to keep the public uninformed. His preferred method was to sue anyone who wrote anything negative about him. Especially when it was true. As much as he delighted in putting his own photo, day after day, on the front pages of his newspapers, he didn't want to see his name next to anything that didn't portray him in the most flattering light.

Seymour M. Hersh, a respected investigative journalist whose awards include a Pulitzer Prize, five George Polk Awards, two National Magazine Awards and a dozen other prizes for his work, was among the writers sued by Maxwell. In his book, *The Samson Option: Israel's Nuclear Arsenal and American Foreign Policy,* published in 1991, he exposed Robert Maxwell and his foreign editor, Nicholas Davies, as being spies for Israel's Mossad.

The libel lawsuit initiated by Robert Maxwell and the Maxwell-owned Mirror Group was settled after his death in Hersh's favor. In a *New York Times* article dated August 19, 1994 headlined *U.S. Author Gets Apology in Libel Case* it states, "Seymour Hersh and his publishers accepted a settlement which consisted of substantial damages and an apology that effectively ended a libel action brought against them in English courts."

Tom Bower, whose many unauthorized biographies of business tycoons have earned him a sterling reputation, was not spared Robert Maxwell's wrath and writs. Bower wrote two books on Maxwell while he was still alive. When *Maxwell: The Outsider* was published, Maxwell sued Bower and his publisher, Aurum Press. They responded by providing proof of everything in the book. While Maxwell did not stop the lawsuit, he let it disappear into the ether. Despite his massive size, Maxwell was a petty man who held grudges. He wasn't going to let Bower make more money from the sale of his book. The hardcover copies sold quite well, however, to ensure the book's circulation was limited, Maxwell purchased the publishing company that held the rights to the paperback edition.

Gordon Thomas was a British investigative journalist who specialized in writing about the Mossad. Martin Dillon, investigative journalist and author, has won international acclaim for his investigative reporting. The two men co-wrote *Robert Maxwell, Israel's Superspy* after Maxwell's death. According to Dillon, Maxwell's family interceded in a bizarre manner. He said the following:

"When my book was published, it received a savage review in the Washington Post by the celebrity lawyer, Alan Dershowitz. That did not come as a shock, but I found it interesting that Dershowitz's personal client and buddy was Jeffrey Epstein whose claimed lover was the New York socialite, Ghislaine Maxwell, daughter of the late Robert Maxwell. I knew that Ghislaine and her sister, Isabel, who was based in San Francisco, were enterprising and highly committed to defending their father's sullied reputation. Prior to my book being published, Isabel had somehow acquired a copy of the manuscript, which had been kept under wraps in New York and London publishers' offices, and ran with it to Israel to present it to her father's friend, Shimon Peres, the former Israeli president, as well as to David Kimche, a former head of Mossad. My co-author, Gordon Thomas, received a call from one of his Mossad sources who had been visited by Isabel Maxwell who demanded that he publicly denounce the book. No one she

approached took the bait. Nevertheless, the pressure on my New York publisher must have been considerable because the book was given almost no publicity when it reached the American market."

The review by Alan Dershowitz hurt book sales in the United States and it appears the Maxwells continued their efforts to suppress that specific book. A recent biography *Fall: The Mystery of Robert Maxwell* was written by one of Ian Maxwell's childhood friends, namely, John Preston.

Preston declares there is nothing to prove Robert Maxwell was a spy in his later years, although he readily admits he was a spy during his early life. The author goes on to describe the larger-than-life press baron as being "too feeble" in his 60s to have been a spy at the time of his death—which is absurd.

Thomas and Dillon interviewed Mossad spy extraordinaire Rafi Eitan who handled Robert Maxwell. They also interviewed other Mossad agents who helped them reconstruct the events leading to what they believe was his murder.

In the same interview Preston begins, "there are several books," he then stops and begins again, "there is one book stating Maxwell was a spy for the Mossad. I don't see anything to support this." He meant Thomas and Dillon's book.

~

What I will show in this book is that the people who inhabited Ghislaine's world were the same as those connected to her father. He made sure to introduce her to his intelligence network. Jeffrey Epstein added his own contacts to the many passed on to Ghislaine vis-à-vis her father. This mix of people from the upper echelons of society co-existed inside the world of spooks, sex, drugs and blackmail.

Bob Fitrakis, who is an investigative journalist, attorney, and professor of Political Science; and who co-authored one of my books *Jeffrey Epstein, Revealed,* wrote a couple of articles in the 1990s on Jeffrey Epstein and Leslie Wexner, CEO of L Brands. L Brands is the holding company for Victoria's Secret, Bath & Body Works, PINK, Neiman-Marcus and, until recently, Bergdorf Goodman. Fitrakis's articles, now scrubbed from the internet, included information about Epstein and Wexner's dealings with the Central Intelligence Agency (CIA).

Among these, the move of the CIA-owned airline, Southern Air Transport (SAT), from Miami, Florida to Rickenbacker International Airport in Columbus, Ohio. This gives credence to Epstein's often repeated claim that he was a spy for the CIA.

A 1986 *Washington Post* article *Ex-CIA Airline Tied to Cocaine* details how a witness told the Federal

Bureau of Investigation (FBI) of having seen an airplane belonging to SAT being used for guns-for-drugs transfer at an airfield in Barranquilla, Columbia.

Jorge Ochoa, a partner of Pablo Escobar, and a member of the Medellin cartel was in charge of the operation. Barry Seal was named by the Drug Enforcement Administration (DEA) as being a pilot for the Ochoa family. They all worked for the CIA—but you won't find a mainstream media article confirming this.

There are clues, however, that show CIA was in bed with the Medellin drug cartel. Specifically, two men who were exposed as being involved in the Iran-Contra affair.

Alan Friers, Jr. and Richard Secord.

Fiers was born in Ohio in 1939 and served as President Ronald Reagan's chief of the CIA's Central American Task Force from 1984 through 1988. When his role in the Iran-Contra scandal was made public, he pleaded guilty to two misdemeanor counts of withholding information from Congress. He served no prison time.

Secord is also an Ohio native, was born in 1932, and worked covert operations with the CIA. He was assigned to Iran where he was in charge of managing all U.S. military assistance to the Iranians. After the covert operation was blown, it was alleged Secord made $2 million on arms transactions. He was subsequently charged with lying to Congress.

Fiers was pardoned by President George H.W. Bush and Secord only received probation.

The New York Times reported in 1995 that the reason for SAT's move from Florida to Ohio was to help Wexner's *The Limited*. The articled cited that SAT was going to help the company get their goods from the Orient into the United States. The *Times* article, which had been readily accessible for 25 years, was scrubbed after the publication of my book *Jeffrey Epstein Predator Spy* in 2020.

SAT was founded in the 1940s and from 1960 through 1973 was directly owned by the CIA. After this they used middlemen, who appeared on the surface to be the owners. However, these were front men, because the CIA still controlled the airline.

In 1982 SAT was exposed as transporting U.S. arms to Iran and goods to the Contras.

When the *Times* article stating Leslie Wexner was utilizing the help of Southern Air Transport went missing, I decided to dig deeper in order to establish the airline had, in fact, been moved to Rickenbacker Port Authority.

I was able to find a government document prepared for the U.S. Army Corps of Engineers in January 2017. The 26-page report commissioned by the United States Army Corps of Engineers (USACE), in coordination with the Ohio Environmental Agency (Ohio EPA), investigated environmental sites known as areas of concern for toxic waste from previous Department of Defense (DOD) operations. Among these areas of concern was the site that had been used by Southern Air Transport during the time of their association with Leslie Wexner's *The Limited*.

Bob Fitrakis received two handwritten letters during the 1990s when he wrote articles about Jeffrey Epstein and Leslie Wexner. The notes were from someone calling himself 'Sky Hawk'. The notes had the same words: "Jeff Epstein = toe tag". Fitrakis took that as a threat.

It wasn't the only warning.

In 2010, author Martin Dillon was approached by a Palm Beach socialite to ask him to write a book on Epstein. The un-named socialite claimed to have a lot of sources within the police department and access to information the public had not seen. She produced phone messages and flight logs which showed Dillon the high-powered world leaders Epstein associated with. She explained the girls were very young – within the ages of 12 to 14. And, she was also very concerned about Ghislaine Maxwell's sexual relationship with them.

One day, the socialite, while in her Manhattan apartment was threatened. Someone used a very powerful laser to put the image of a penis on her bedroom ceiling. She became terrified and immediately called Dillon frantically explaining to him it was Epstein's egg-shaped penis.

He was skeptical of her statement and wondered if she was to be trusted at all. To investigate further, Dillon contacted a person he knows in the intelligence community. His contact told him it would require scoping out her apartment, and that a laser like that only exists within the Industrial Military Complex. He concluded that whoever did this had to have very "serious friends".

And, there was yet another threat.

Graydon Carter, former Vanity Fair editor, reported that back in 2006, as the feds compiled accusations against Jeffrey Epstein in Palm Beach, Florida he sent John Connolly, a contributing editor for the magazine to investigate the story. As Connolly began to interview the victims who had been lured into Epstein's teenage sex trafficking ring Carter called him to report he'd found the severed head of a cat in the front yard of his

Connecticut home. "It was done to intimidate. No question about it."

Connolly decided to stop reporting on Epstein and Maxwell and later penned the best-seller *Filthy Rich* with James Patterson. *Filthy Rich* also became a widely viewed Netflix documentary. This wasn't the first threat Carter received. There had been another after in 2003 after Vicky Ward's *The Talented Mr. Epstein.* Immediately upon publication he found a bullet just outside the door of his Manhattan home.

The threats against Carter continued. In 2006 Bill Clinton and Prince Andrew warned him directly that if he proceeded to write another story on Epstein, they would shutter his new restaurant in Greenwich Village.

Needless to say journalists and writers who publish anything on Epstein and Maxwell are being watched.

On June 2, 2021 after one of the chapters of this book showing a young Ghislaine partying in London in the 1980s was excerpted in *The Steeple Times,* Isabel Maxwell pre-ordered it through my website.

PROLOGUE

The Suicide of Genius

———————————

Genius was the Maxwell family's butler at Headington Hill Hall just before Robert Maxwell disappeared at sea. He was given this name which the Maxwells and their friends used when speaking to him because Robert Maxwell thought him to be "proverbially thick".

By way of example when asked why he referred to his butler as *Genius* Bob would tell the tale that he'd asked him to serve rosé wine and Genius poured into the flute-like stemmed Venetian glasses red and white wine together making it look as if it were rosé.

"No, no, no, no," Maxwell recalled yelling at him. "Not like that. Find a bottle of rosé wine which someone delivered to the house in a crate and start again."

The Maxwells treated their staff as if they inhabited the world of Victorian England one hundred years earlier. Household help were under constant scrutiny, distrusted, and always being reminded they were not members of the family. They were expected to make themselves silent and invisible. If they couldn't remember their names the Maxwells simply assigned them one.

Genius had not been working too long at Headington Hill Hall when he stepped out of the house one day and greeted Robert Maxwell who was wearing his favorite pale blue suit with a starched white shirt and his signature red bow tie.

In the butler's hand was a recently sharpened meat clever. He carefully rolled up his sleeve, ignoring for once the glaring eyes of his boss, and slashed his wrist. Blood splattered everywhere—much of it landing on Maxwell's blue suit.

Maxwell was silent for a few seconds and before the man's body fell to the ground he said, "Genius, what you did shows you to be very brave, but also very stupid."

When the authorities arrived to pick up the corpse they were told by the family and friends that Genius was very likely suicidal because he probably realized he was in the wrong job.

ONE

Virginia Roberts, 1999

———

Cereal heiress Marjorie Merriweather Post built the acre estate known as Mar-a-Lago in Palm Beach, Florida in 1924. The 11,000 square foot oceanfront house has 58 bedrooms and 33 bathrooms. It was designed to look like a European palace and it was her desire that it become a retreat for U.S. Presidents.

In 1980, the estate with Spanish-Moorish architecture was declared a National Historic Landmark. It was purchased in 1985 by Donald Trump for $10 million. Trump turned it into a country club for the impossibly rich, and in a tradition not well received in Palm Beach, he even welcomed the nouveau riche.

The impeccably dressed woman with short cropped black hair and dark brown eyes was a regular at the exclusive Palm Beach resort. Her proper British accent added to the aura of money and confidence she exuded. It was at Mar-a-Lago in the summer of 2000 that Ghislaine Maxwell would meet and befriend 16-year-old Virginia Roberts who had just taken on a summer job as a locker room assistant.

Virginia's life had been difficult. At 11 her mother had decided she was out of control and placed her in a state-run juvenile delinquent facility. One would lead to another, but they were all the same: full of violence. Constant fights would break out several times every week between the rougher girls with the staff using pepper spray and strip searches to subdue them. In a court document Virginia said, "every girl was treated like a violent criminal."

At 13, she ran away only to find herself in the clutches of a pedophile trafficker named Ron Eppinger.

In addition to viciously raping her on a regular basis, Eppinger sold her repeatedly to other men. By the time Virginia was 15 she had gotten re-united with her parents, enrolled herself in school to get a GED, and was grateful that her dad, who worked at Mar-a-Lago, had been able to put in a good word for her to land a summer job. Life was beginning to look normal again for the young girl who had lost touch with what normal looked like. Virginia even had a plan for the future. She was going to become a massage therapist, and to prepare, began studying books on anatomy.

On a quiet Tuesday afternoon in June, while at work, Virginia was immersed in one of her anatomy books, when the dark-haired lady with the English accent in her late thirties asked her a question. To Virginia's surprise the woman took an interest in her.

"Do you also massage people on the side?" she asked her lips broadening into a Cheshire grin.

"No, I'm just reading the book, but one day I would love to practice massage therapy," Virginia answered.

"Well, it's lovely to meet you. My name is Ghislaine Maxwell," she extended her hand.

"My name is Jenna, nice to meet you," Virginia responded while pointing to the nametag on her shirt. "Would you care for something to drink?"

"Tea would be lovely," Ghislaine replied.

The older woman began to tell her about the rich man she worked for named Jeffrey. "He's looking for a massage therapist," she added as she took another sip of her tea. "I could introduce you to him."

"No, I don't know the body well enough to even try to a job interview," Virginia replied.

"That shouldn't be a problem. If he likes you, he will see to it you get the best training in the industry. After all, you've got such a cheery disposition. I can see by the sticky notes in your book that you're an enthusiastic learner. Here, take my number," Ghislaine reached into her bag and pulled out one of her cards she kept for precisely one of these moments.

Before saying their goodbyes, Ghislaine obtained a promise from Virginia that she would drop by Jeffrey Epstein's house, not far from Mar-a-Lago, after work later in the day.

At 5 p.m. Virginia's father drove her to the house on the dead-end street on El Brillo Way near the Palm Beach intercoastal. Behind the wooden doors Virginia saw the large pink mansion and was filled with excitement.

"Wish me luck, dad," she said and he gave her a squeeze telling her he wished her the best.

Ghislaine greeted them shaking her father's hand and thanking him for bringing her. She then kissed them both on the cheek in the way the French Europeans do.

"The boss is waiting for you upstairs," she said prompting Virginia to say goodbye to her father and follow the older woman up the stairs.

On their way Virginia noticed a couple of long hall tables full of photos of young and beautiful girls. Many of them wearing only a smile. At the top of the stairs they made a right. The lights were dimmed in the bedroom but Virginia could still see the king size bed in the middle of the room. Ghislaine glided past the bed and Virginia followed her into a smaller room beyond it to the massage room.

It was as extravagantly furnished as Mar-a-Lago with marble walls, a glass-enclosed shower, a self-automated steam room and wall-to-wall Burberry carpeting.

A naked man was lying down on top of a turquoise massage table. She heard Ghislaine's voice introduce her to the man.

Jeffrey Epstein glanced up and looked her over giving Ghislaine a smile of approval.

"Just call me Jeffrey, no need for formalities," he said with a grin.

"Treat this as a lesson and follow my lead," Ghislaine directed. "If you do well then maybe you can become Jeffrey's travelling masseuse, see the world and get paid well for it."

Ghislaine walked over to the sink and began to wash her hands and Virginia followed listening attentively to her instructions.

"Always keep one hand on Jeffrey, even when getting more lotion. This way it won't make him lose concentration and he will remain relaxed."

Feeling grateful, Virginia nodded enthusiastically. She couldn't believe her luck. "Ok," she replied.

"Oh, a tip," Ghislaine added reassured the girl was going to work out just fine. "Always keep a blob of lotion high up on your forearm so that it is less disruptive for Jeffrey."

These were good lessons, Virginia thought silently as she followed Ghislaine back to Jeffrey who was patiently waiting on the massage table.

Virginia mimicked Ghislaine's movements and they both began to massage his feet beginning with his heels and then into the arches of his soles. Their hands moved in unison as they began to push up on his calves and then repeated the motion. Virginia was enjoying her first lesson in learning how the body worked and once again couldn't believe her luck that she was learning all of this for free.

Then the questions began. Jeffrey and Ghislaine asked her all about her life and feeling like she could trust them, she opened up and told them about the horrible situation with Ron. This piqued their curiosity even further and they asked more questions without even sounding surprised at everything she'd revealed to them. Instead it seemed like they were entertained by her sad life up to that moment.

"Naughty-girl," Jeffrey chided with a mischievous smile.

"No, I'm not," Virginia retorted in her defense. "I'm really a good girl, just always in the wrong places."

"That's okay, I like naughty girls."

Jeffrey then rolled over on his back and exposed himself. He had a full erection.

Taken by surprise, Virginia turned to get a cue from Ghislaine, but to her surprise saw she had removed her top and was standing behind her bare breasted.

Before Virginia could even begin to think about what was happening, Ghislaine began to undress her. Jeffrey was loving every minute of it and had begun to stroke himself as he leered at her.

Then, as if she were on another planet, she heard them joke about her little girl panties.

After being raped and still smarting from the humiliation of being reduced, once again, to a piece of flesh for the use of other people, she was led into the steam room. Ghislaine left her and Epstein alone so that she could continue to obey his every wish.

Epstein instructed her not to say anything to anyone about what just happened. And then he boasted that he's made billions of dollars going from being a middle-class professor to an elite financial advisor for clients with over one billion dollars in their bank. Virginia can barely absorb everything he is saying when she hears him ask her to help him shower.

She was humiliated and disappointed. This was not how she had envisioned the interview to turn out. Instead of giving in to the trickle of tears she tried to console herself with the thought that there was no running away from the sick world she once again found herself in. Perhaps this was the way it was supposed to be.

～

In a 2011 profile about how Maxwell was welcomed back into society after Epstein was jailed, one unnamed insider said of Maxwell:

"She's a high-end fixer, and so what? No one in café society gives a damn that a 15-year-old girl gives massages.

"She gets people into parties and runs around for a lot of people.

"If you're Mike Huckabee it would matter but not if you're Ghislaine Maxwell."

On January 2015 Buckingham Palace issued a statement denying allegations that Prince Andrew had sex with Virginia. "Any suggestion of impropriety with underage minors is categorically untrue…it is emphatically denied that the Duke of York had any form of sexual contact or relationship with Virginia Roberts. The allegations made are false and without any foundation."

Maxwell, for her part, gave an interview calling Roberts a liar.

Virginia Roberts who now goes by her married name Giuffre sued her for defamation.

The lawsuit was settled by Ghislaine Maxwell in 2017. Maxwell paid Virginia Giuffre an unspecified amount of money.

TWO

Ghislaine Maxwell, 2016

––––––––––––

Ghislaine Maxwell was considered among her peers as one of their own: a *socialite.* Even after she was exposed for having been the madam for Jeffrey Epstein's child sex trafficking ring, few turned their backs on her. To them she did nothing wrong.

One of her friends told a reporter that no one in café society gives a damn about a 15-year-old girl giving massages. He added, "She [Ghislaine] gets people into parties and runs around for a lot. If you're Mike Huckabee it would matter but not if you're Ghislaine Maxwell."

Ghislaine was the favorite daughter of the late Robert Maxwell whose thieving ways earned him the moniker "Crook of the Century". And, apparently the elite were fine with his daughter's unseemly side.

Her accusers share a different view.

The women who allege they were procured as teenagers or young women, then raped by her and Epstein know her best.

In Ghislaine's younger years, she was charming with many friends and admirers. What started her down the path of darkness was vanity and greed. She wanted to continue to be rich after her father's sudden death left the family in dire financial straits. She didn't know how to achieve this on her own. There was no switch that was flipped. The lights just slowly faded into darkness as she became the female embodiment of her devious father.

Johanna Sjoberg was a college student in Florida in 2001 when she was allegedly recruited by Ghislaine. Maxwell lured her to Epstein's Palm Beach estate under the guise she of working as a personal assistant. Almost immediately Johanna realized her job was to provide sexual massages. She was tersely told by Ghislaine that Epstein needed three orgasms a day. When Johanna failed to achieve this Ghislaine punished her.

Court documents reveal that a 15-year-old Swedish girl was held against her will at Jeffrey Epstein's private island, known as "Orgy Island" as a sex slave. Upon arrival the first thing Ghislaine did was to collect every girl's passport.

Rinaldo Rizzo, a former house manager for Glenn and Eva Andersson-Dubin, described his encounter with the teenager in his employers' kitchen. In excerpts of a 2016 deposition Rizzo said she was "distraught and shaking...literally quivering" as she described her treatment at Maxwell's hands.

He added, "She sat in the stool exactly the way the girls that I mentioned to you sat at Jeffrey's house, with no expression and with their head down,"

When Eva left the kitchen Rizzo and his wife introduced themselves tentatively to the distraught teenager.

In the deposition Rizzo recalls the events of that morning:

"She doesn't really respond. Nothing verbal, no cues, her head is still down. I asked her if she would like some water, tissue, anything, and she basically doesn't respond."

He decided to make small talk in an effort to calm her down.

"Oh, by the way, do you work for Jeffrey?"

"Yes."

"What do you do?"

"I'm Jeffrey Epstein's executive assistant, his personal assistant," she replied.

This puzzled him as she seemed too young for a position like that, and so he asked her age and how she got the job.

Rizzo continues:

"And she says to me, point blank, 'I'm 15,' and I said to her you're 15-years-old and you have a position like that?" At that point she just breaks down hysterical and I feel like I just said something wrong, and she will not stop crying.

"And then in a state of shock, she just lets it rip, and what she told me was unbelievable…She proceeded to tell my wife and I…'I was on the island and there was Ghislaine and there was Sarah,' and then she said, 'They asked me for sex. I said no.'"

Rizzo explained that when she refused to have sex, Sarah Kellen took her phone and passport and gave them to Ghislaine.

"And at that point she said she was threatened," Rizzo testified. "And I said, 'Threatened?' She says, 'Yes, I was threatened by Ghislaine not to discuss this.'"

Rizzo said the girl stopped talking when she heard someone approach the kitchen.

"Eva comes in and tells her that she will be working for her in the city as a nanny."

Rizzo said he saw the girl one other time approximately one month later aboard a flight with the Dubin family to Sweden. And, that based on what he was told she was dropped off at a Swedish airport.

According to the 2015 defamation lawsuit initiated by Virginia Giuffre (nee Roberts) against Ghislaine Maxwell, Virginia alleged she was Epstein and Maxwell's sex slave. She explained that after they trained her, she was handed commercial airline tickets and sent to the Dubins at their hotel. She explained that she had sex with Glenn in one room while his pregnant wife, Eva, slept in the other. Virginia described the Dubins as her "tester couple".

It should be noted that Glenn Dubin is not a pop star, nor is he a household name. The fact that a teenager was able to know their names and location is too detailed to be anything but the truth.

In 2006 Sarah Ransome was 22 when recruited by Natalya Malyshev who is alleged to be one of many recruiters employed by Epstein and Maxwell. Ransome alleges Ghislaine taught her how to sexually pleasure Epstein. The devilish duo promised to send her to the Fashion Institute of Technology (FIT). However, in order to reap the benefit of their connections she was told she had to comply with their sexual demands.

Ransome asserts that the couple make it clear to her that while they had the ability to advance her career, they also had the ability to make sure she would obtain no formal education or modeling agency contracts if she failed to provide sexual favors. (Case 1:17-cv-00616-JGK Filed 01/26/17). Ransome was provided a cell phone and an apartment at 301 East 66th Street in Manhattan. In an interview with one of the reporters covering the Jeffrey Epstein story, she said, "You know, when Jeffrey wanted me, you know, Sarah Kellen or Ghislaine would call me into his bedroom and I had no choice but to go."

She added, "Ghislaine Maxwell treated her sex slaves like the shit on her shoe."

On February 16, 2021 Ira Rosen, producer for *60 Minutes*, published a new memoir titled *Ticking Clock*. In the book Rosen claims that early in 2016 he tricked Ghislaine Maxwell into confirming the sex tapes existed. Rosen describes meeting with her at a restaurant in New York City and, acting on a hunch, he said flatly, "I want the tapes of [Donald] Trump with the girls."

Maxwell replied, "I don't know where they are."

"Ask Epstein," he urged and added, "the fate of the country is at stake. Trump could be elected president and how would you feel if those tapes emerged after he was in office?"

Maxwell gave him a stern look and then pointed a finger at his face.

"I am the daughter of a press baron. I know the way you people think. If you do one side, you must do the other. If you get the tapes on Trump you have to do Clinton."

Of note, Maxwell remains a close friend of Bill and Hillary Clinton. Her relationship with the Clintons goes back many decades. A photo surfaced showing Maxwell in attendance at Chelsea Clinton's wedding in 2010. The Clintons told the press it was their daughter's wedding and that only those closest to her would be invited. The saying "A picture is worth a thousand words" was never truer than what this image conveyed.

Rosen replied, "I will go wherever the story goes."

Maxwell told him that Epstein never told her the whereabouts of the tapes.

Rosen writes, "Maxwell didn't want Trump elected, but said Hillary Clinton was comfortably ahead and there was no need for the story to come out."

He believes wealthy men in Palm Beach invested with Jeffrey Epstein after being extorted with pictures from nights of debauchery.

～

Among the people who claim Epstein and Maxwell had surveillance cameras is Virginia Giuffre. Giuffre is the most out-spoken victim and in 2015 sued Ghislaine Maxwell for defamation. The lawsuit was settled by Maxwell in 2017. One of the documents Giuffre provided to the court was her never published memoir. She writes:

"We found Ghislaine where we had left her, in her office. She had just received an order, a satellite camera with a twelve-inch flat screen. She told us how it was used to pick up any person in any location with the quick insert of an address. Quite a powerful new toy I thought, but it was only a minute display of what the rich could afford, what use they would get out of it was another concern. Soon after she was done figuring out the controls on the camera, we made a rare and first for me pit stop, the security room. What I thought was our way out by the front door was another hidden door. I was in shock as I was led into a room, so discreet that in three years I never even knew it existed. I kept my head down most of the time, knowing how secretive this must

be. It was an entire security base within his mansion. What I could see when I stole a glimpse here and there was an array of tiny screens, twenty odd or something. Small screens showing various rooms of the mansion I had recognized. The images were constantly changing so I found it hard to pinpoint an exact location but from the decor and short glimpses I suddenly knew from then on that my feelings of my every move being watched inside his corridors was now more than a possibility but was actually happening. Jeffrey spoke to an obese Spanish guy at the desk, whose job was to disgustingly overlook all of the video feedback."

Maria Farmer worked for Jeffrey Epstein in 1996 as the door person at his mansion in Manhattan. She claims Epstein showed her the extensive secret camera system where he secretly recorded private moments with hidden pinhole cameras in bedrooms and even bathrooms.

"I looked on the cameras, and I saw toilet, toilet, bed, bed, toilet, bed," she said. "I'm like, I am never gonna use the restroom here and I'm never gonna sleep here, you know what I mean? It was very obvious that they were like monitoring private moments."

In the summer of 1996 Jeffrey Epstein sent Maria to Leslie Wexner's guesthouse in Ohio as an artist in residence. During Epstein and Maxwell's third visit the pair attempted to entice her into a threesome.

When Maxwell was told by Vicky Ward (a writer for *Vanity Fair* and a friend of hers) that Farmer had reported her and the rest of the people involved to the FBI, Maxwell began to make threatening phone calls. Farmer claims she has been in hiding for many years because Ghislaine kept threatening her life. "Most of her threats were veiled. She warned me, 'You better look over your shoulder because there's someone coming for you.'"

In a deposition Farmer said Ghislaine Maxwell told her, "We're going to burn all your art. And I just want you to know that anything you ever make will be burned. Your career is burned. I know you go to the West Side Highway all the time. While you're out there, just be really careful because there are a lot of ways to die there."

≈

There is an allegation from one of the victims who mistakenly opened the door of the surveillance room and caught Epstein and Maxwell watching a video of Prince Andrew having sex with one of the minor girls. The Duke of York vehemently denied allegations he had sex with Virginia. Despite this, on February 15, 2022 headlines around the world read, *Britain's Prince Andrew has settled a New York federal lawsuit that accused him of sexually assaulting a leading accuser of his friend Jeffrey Epstein while she was underage.*

David Boies, who represented dozens of Epstein's victims said, "Jeffrey Epstein had surveillance in his homes in New York and Palm Beach." He stated that Prince Andrew would have appeared on a very large quantity of tapes. According to him, other well-known men were also caught on camera. Among these: former Israeli Prime Minister Ehud Barak, Harvard professor Alan Dershowitz and former Senator George Mitchell.

A 1996 *New York Times* article entitled *Home Sweet Elsewhere* mentioned the surveillance system at the Manhattan mansion Leslie Wexner purchased and which Jeffrey Epstein called home.

Visitors described a bathroom reminiscent of James Bond movies: hidden beneath a stairway, lined with lead to provide shelter from attack and supplied with closed-circuit television screens and a telephone, both concealed in a cabinet beneath the sink. The house also has a heated sidewalk, a luxurious provision that explains why, while snow blankets the rest of the Eastern Seaboard, the Wexner house (and Bill Cosby's house across the street) remains opulently snow-free, much to the delight of neighborhood dogs.

Many of Epstein and Maxwell's victims said their relationship with not a boyfriend, girlfriend but more like brother, sister.

In Virginia Giuffre's manuscript submitted to the court during the defamation lawsuit against Maxwell, she writes,

"I couldn't understand why Ghislaine and Jeffrey had such an openly intimate relationship but yet never regarded themselves as partners. They rarely kissed and never held hands or even slept in the same bed. It was more like a sexual arrangement between the two of them. She brings in the girls for his particular taste and he supplies to lavish lifestyle she was accustomed to before her family lost all of their fortune."

The victims have all echoed the same complaint. That Maxwell sexually abused them as much as Epstein.

THREE

Robert Maxwell, the Early Years

By the time Ghislaine Maxwell was born on December 25, 1961 Robert Maxwell had been a spy since the second World War. His cover as a publishing mogul and owner of Maxwell Communications Corporate (MCC) was how he was viewed by the world.

Under this corporate umbrella he would place his holdings: Pergamon Press, Macmillan McGraw Hill,

Mirror Group, Berlitz International and an assortment of others as the opportunity arose.

Victor Ostrovsky, a former Mossad officer, would later claim the Mossad was funding its operations in Europe from the money they stole from Maxwell's newspaper pension fund. As soon as Robert Maxwell accepted money from the Mossad to purchase the *Mirror Newspaper Group* – it was under their control as well as the man himself. Maxwell had set out to build a media empire but ended up living his life like a John le Carré villain chasing spies across the globe.

Born on June 10, 1923 into a poor Jewish family in the village of Solotvina—in what was then Czechoslovakia—Robert Maxwell was one of seven children. His parents were Mechel Hoch and Hannah Slomowitz and they lived in a two-room wooden shack with an earthen-floor. Their firstborn was Brana, followed by Abrahaim Lein (later known as Robert Maxwell), followed by Chaim, Shenie, Sylvia, Zissel and Cipra. Two of the children died in infancy of pneumonia for which there was no medicine at the time. For the remaining children it meant a little more food and more room in the one bed they shared.

In 1919 the Hoch family name was replaced with Ludvik as Europe realigned after World War One. When it was time to register Maxwell's birth, his parents were advised that it was important for him to have an undisputed Czech name. And, so they added Jan before Abraham, and changed Hoch to Ludvik. For years, he was known as Jan Abraham Ludvik.

His mother, whom he loved dearly and spoke fondly of throughout his life, was a political activist and a believer in Zionism. Zionism is a movement to re-establish a Jewish nation in Palestine. She is the reason he claimed to be a staunch Zionist, although he didn't openly declare this until later in life. He denied his Jewish roots, married a French woman of Protestant descent, who had an upper-class upbringing and settled into high society in London.

Maxwell's mother taught him to read and by the time he was 10 he could write better than his father. It was not the norm for women to be educated in those days. One of his nephews remembered that she "picked up every piece of newspaper in the street to discover what was going on." Another relative recalls she was "an exception in the village because she read books. She was almost an intellectual." And yet another remembered her as "an exemplary cook of kosher food."

It was from his adoring mother that Maxwell claimed to have inherited his insatiable ambition. It was from her, he insisted, that he learned the importance of mastering different languages. He would become fluent in nine.

Her words of advice to her beloved son in a world not accommodating to Jews was, "Try not to look so Jewish." And so he dropped Abraham from his name and became simply Jan Ludvick. Anti-Semitism was everywhere with Hitler filling the airwaves with demands for *"lebensraum"*. It was the idea that land expansion was essential to the survival of the German people. By 1938 Sudentenland, which was the German speaking part of Czechoslovakia, fell under Nazi control. The Munich agreement of September 30, 1938 (agreed upon by Germany, the French Third Republic and Italy) allowed "cession to Germany of the Sudeten Germany territory" of Czechoslovakia. And so, the country of Maxwell's birth fell under Nazi control too.

His mother had instilled in him that "to behave and act like an Englishman is to be successful." These were the words he never forgot and the advice that helped him rise to the top of British society. He would deny his Jewish heritage until almost the end of his life.

At the age of 16, with only three years of formal education, he left home to join the resistance against the Nazis in 1940. Arriving in Marseille he joined the Czechoslovak army and when France fell he marched on to the United Kingdom where and became a proud member of the British Army.

The ambitious young man had grown tall with movie star good looks. His jet-back hair, olive complexion and commanding demeanor captivated men and women alike. Always trying to improve himself, he persuaded a local woman to help him learn proper English.

She taught him the difference between vowels and consonants and taught him the proper etiquette required of an English gentleman. Among these, that if seated, a man always stood up when a woman entered the room; that milk is always poured first; and, that tea is never slurped. She taught him how to play whist and dominoes – the popular forms of social entertainment in England at the time. She even taught him how to dance and the art of small talk which he appears not to have mastered.

He was hungry for learning and picked up any scrap of newspaper on the street reading them voraciously which is a habit he acquired from his mother. To hone his sense of humor he listened to radio comedy shows. *It's that Man Again* (ITMA) was his favorite. ITMA was considered to have contributed to maintaining the morale of the British people during the war. It had a cheerful take on the day-to-day lives of the characters. The central role belonged to a fast-talking man around whom the other characters orbited. He was someone, undoubtedly, who Maxwell began to emulate. Being the center of everyone's attention was where Maxwell felt he belonged. Perhaps it reminded him of the attention his mother bestowed upon him creating for him a bubble of unconditional love and safety. He would be okay, he would succeed – he knew this because his mother told him he could do anything.

Maxwell went on to fight in the Normandy invasion and across Europe, becoming a decorated war hero.

Through the Red Cross in 1943 Maxwell received the last letter he would ever get from his mother saying she was well.

In 1944 most of his family was killed at Auschwitz—a complex of over 40 concentration and extermination camps operated by Nazi Germany. He would not learn about this until after the war when he met with two of his sisters who were liberated from one of the camps. They told him how the family had been taken away and driven straight to Auschwitz in July 1944. There, his parents with five of his sisters and brothers, were gassed. Maxwell would forever mourn this tragic loss and would, upon marrying, attempt to recreate the family lost to Hitler's Third Reich.

To improve himself he began to imitate the speech and mannerisms of the wealthy. Some of the many aliases he used had an air of aristocracy to them although they often sprang from childish notions. For example. Robert Maxwell used the alias Leslie Du

Maurier. A name he obtained from Du Maurier cigarettes which he became aware of during his time in France.

One of Maxwell's early affairs was with a nurse whose parents were wealthy and part of the refined world of the English upper class. It was wartime Europe and they turned a blind eye to their suspicion that he was sleeping with their daughter. Their relationship lasted for two years. It was during this time that Maxwell soaked up their manner, language and behavior. He copied them as if he were a portrait painter. Except that he was the canvas and they were the paint. He would later tell close associates that he "acquired the polish he lacked" in their home listening to their stories while bedding their daughter. Although he was self-congratulatory believing himself to be flawless to others his polish was not deep. It evaporated quickly despite first impressions.

Maxwell's first love would describe him in later years as "enchanting, fascinating and infuriating". She claimed he was either exuberant or in the depths of melancholy. It was through her that he was introduced into the world of England's upper class. Emboldened by this relationship and his new contacts, he sent a letter to the Sixth Battalion, which made its way up to the regiment's commanding officer. Impressed with his language skills and war experience, they placed him in the regiment's 17th Infantry Brigade's intelligence unit.

Records show he was a good sniper and an excellent interrogator. When he questioned German prisoners he referred to himself as Leslie Jones.

Just before his 21st birthday he was once again promoted. His commanding officer suggested that neither alias Maxwell had at the time, du Maurier or Jones, were suitable for an officer and a gentleman in the North Shaffs. A more appropriate one, he advised should connote a Scottish ancestry.

His ego had become as large as the whole of England and so he selected Maxwell, after the well-bred aristocratic Maxwell family of Caelaverock Castle. From this moment on he would be known to the world as Robert Maxwell.

Maxwell had risen effortlessly through the military ranks. First as a 16-year-old who'd lied proclaiming to be 19 and achieving the rank of sergeant. In 1945 he was promoted once again – this time to captain. In the same year his heroism won him the Military Cross. And while Maxwell showed no fear on the battlefield, even risking his life to carry a fellow soldier over his shoulder to safety, he also became known as a ruthless killer.

Fellow solders dubbed him "Killer Maxwell" for the pleasure he appeared to take in killing captured

Germans. This abandonment of reason and civility would come back to haunt him in later years. Before his death in 1991 Robert Maxwell came under scrutiny for alleged war crimes. During one of the many interviews Maxwell gave he'd boasted that in April 1945 while serving in the British Army as captain he had shot dead the mayor of a German town.

In Joe Haine's second book on Robert Maxwell simply titled *Maxwell,* he writes that Maxwell shot the mayor who approached him while under a white flag because "the Germans had done the same to members of his unit."

Controversy, success and failure would be his lifelong companions.

Maxwell never forgot the poverty from whence he came. In later years, he shared the memories which he fought hard to conceal during his youth. Once he was ensconced in the rarified world of power and money—only then did he speak openly about his impoverished childhood:

"We took turns to wear a pair shoes to school in the morning and another of us walked home in them. We carried newspaper to stuff them to adjust the foot size."

And to his own family in later years, he revealed:

"We were very poor. We didn't have the things that other people had. They had shoes and food and we didn't. At the end of the war. I discovered the fate of my

parents and my sisters and brothers, relatives and neighbors. I don't know what went through their minds as they realized they had been tricked into a gas chamber."

In September 1944, he met his future wife, former school teacher, Elisabeth Maynard, in the newly liberated Paris.

For official reasons, he was given the address of the offices of the Paris Welcome Committee located at the Place de la Madeleine. He was greeted by a friendly 23-year-old petite brunette. Elisabeth, known to all as Betty, worked for the Committee as an interpreter. She would later tell their children it was love at first sight; that she swooned and Maxwell, believing she was hungry, took her to lunch.

Shortly thereafter, on March 15, 1945 the two married.

The Ides of March – March 15 – is considered by many to be unlucky. Julius Caesar was stabbed as many as 23 times on this day in 44 BC. Bad luck would follow Mr. & Mrs. Maxwell for the duration of their marriage and beyond.

During an interview later in life he was asked if there was anything he was afraid of. His forehead creasing, he stared at the journalist and stated, "Yes, lack of time." It would prove to be a most prophetic answer.

~

On Christmas 1946 a young Robert Maxwell, his new wife Betty and their first-born Michael pose for the camera. She is reclining on top of a baby grand piano next to which stands a tall festive Christmas tree. Their baby boy is seated in front of her and the dashing young father, sporting a trim mustache and wearing a pinstriped suit with a fashionable polka dot tie, stands beside them beaming with pride. The young couple stare lovingly into each other's eyes.

Soon their lives will be met by tragedy.

They would have nine children: Michael, Philip, Anne, fraternal twins Christine and Isabel, Karine, Ian, Kevin and Ghislaine. Karine died at age three of leukemia and their firstborn, Michael, was in an accident at the age of 15 just three days before Ghislaine's birth in 1961. He was in a coma for seven years and died without ever regaining consciousness in 1969.

Three-year-old Ghislaine, feeling ignored by her grieving parents, complained to her mother, "Mummy, I exist."

Those who knew her as a little girl said she was spoiled and demanding. Maxwell believed one is either a predator or a victim. He had no tolerance for anyone who didn't push back. The couple's youngest child learned this lesson from her earliest days.

FOUR

J. Edgar Hoover

J. Edgar Hoover, who for 37 years reigned unchecked as the director of the FBI, was born on New Year's Day in 1895. His parents were middle class Protestants who lived in a neighborhood known as Seward Square just three blocks behind the Capitol.

Both of them were civil servants who worked for the U.S. government.

He was an only child and his parents settled on calling him Edgar ignoring his given name: John. At the age of five he developed a stutter which he overcame by teaching himself to talk quickly. In high school he joined the debate team and argued against a woman's right to vote and defended his belief in the death penalty. Wanting to enter politics, Hoover began working for the Library of Congress while attending George Washington University Law School at night.

His uncle helped him get a draft-exempt job at the Justice Department's War Emergency Division at the beginning of World War I. The division, commencing in 1903, had been collecting and maintaining secret files on private citizens engaged in what was perceived as radical politics. It was here in this little-known civilian monitoring branch that J. Edgar Hoover learned all manner of espionage, blackmail and secrecy.

Although his father, who suffered bouts of mental illness died in 1921, Hoover continued to live with his morally righteous and domineering mother until her death in 1938. At the tender age of 29, in 1924, Hoover was appointed the first director of the Federal Bureau of Investigation by President Calvin Coolidge.

The young Hoover was awkward with women and led a deeply repressed sexual life. Jimmy Corcoran, a former Bureau Inspector and trusted associate had been asked by Hoover to help him with a serious problem. He had been arrested on sex charges in New Orleans involving a boy. Corcoran was able to hush the matter up. Throughout his life Hoover cross-dressed, dallied with teenage boys, and was one of many famous men identified by minors during a pedophile investigation in Los Angeles.

He was happy to be surrounded by a cadre of handsome young FBI agents – all of whom were men as no women were allowed until 1972. When he met Clyde Tolson he became besotted.

Tolson had become an FBI agent in 1928 and two years later Hoover made him the second-ranking official in the agency creating the title of Associate Director to distinguish him from the others. They shared their meals together twice every day, went on joint vacations, dressed alike and were inseparable. When Edgar was invited to someone's home for dinner, Clyde was promptly issued an invitation as well. In this way they were recognized as a couple by the people in their circle. This was a time in history when sex between men was illegal carrying with it a tremendous amount of social stigma.

This aspect of Hoover's life as head of a federal government agency while simultaneously thumbing his nose at the law speaks volumes about his personal abuse of power.

Compromising photographs of J. Edgar Hoover with Clyde Tolson began surfacing within the gay community in 1948. Author Anthony Summers writes in his book, *Official and Confidential: The Secret Life of J. Edgar Hoover:*

"Top organized crime figures Meyer Lansky and Frank Costello obtained photos of Hoover's homosexual activity with longtime aide Clyde Tolson and used them to blackmail him to ensure the FBI didn't target their illegal activities."

It is alleged Lansky and Costello got the incriminating photographs from William Donovan during one of his feuds with Hoover. Donovan was chief of the Office of Strategic Services (OSS) the precursor of the Central Intelligence Agency (CIA).

The damning blackmail material was held over Hoover's head during the 37 years he reigned as Director. He never went after the mob or interfered in the business of the CIA.

Over a decade later when John F. Kennedy was assassinated in 1963 after his brother, Bobby, took on the mob, Hoover privately gloated. While he didn't have the charm of the Kennedys, nor their good looks, he certainly had the street smarts to keep himself alive. The bad blood that existed between the Kennedys and Hoover was based on his refusal to go after organized crime. While Kennedy was in office he kept the powerful family under his thumb with files composed of their kinky sex romps, bribery, murders and acts he considered treasonous.

Hoover knew firsthand the value of sexual blackmail as a powerful weapon and just like he taught himself to stop stuttering he taught himself how to become a master blackmailer. For this he kept a large cache of secret files on presidents, senators, congressmen, Supreme Court judges, celebrities and anyone who wielded power.

In *Secrets of the FBI* by Ronald Kessler writes:

"The moment [Hoover] would get something on a senator," said William Sullivan, who became the number three official in the bureau under Hoover, "he'd send one of the errand boys up and advise the senator that 'we're in the course of an investigation, and we by chance happened to come up with this data on your daughter. But we wanted you to know this. We realize you'd want to know it.' Well, Jesus, what does that tell the senator? From that time on, the senator's right in his pocket."

On April 1, 1954 a 30-year-old man, with an almost olive complexion, slightly receding black hair, a little over 6 feet tall, weighing approximately 215 pounds, wearing a dark blue suit, a light blue shirt, and sporting a black Homburg hat arrived at Idlewild airport in New York City making his way to The Plaza hotel in midtown Manhattan.

The staff whispered amongst each other as they knew him from earlier trips. Some disliked him more than others because of his intense arrogance. They braced themselves for his two-day visit. Perhaps this is why they were so accommodating when they were recruited by one of Hoover's men to supply even the smallest of details about the imposing dark-haired man with the olive complexion.

They had been watching Maxwell's every step as he was considered to be a person of interest and of concern for national security. J. Edgar Hoover had amassed everything there was to know about him. He had been born on June 10, 1923 in Czechoslovakia, served in the British Army during World War II, became a naturalized British subject, and was issued British passport number 507441 in London on August 12, 1953.

When Maxwell arrived at Idlewood earlier in the day he had been questioned by one of the inspectors. In a composed, but well-rehearsed flurry, he answered the questions in a deep booming voice with a clipped British accent typical of the British upper class. "Yes, my first name is Enian and England has been my residence since birth." The inspector would take note again that Maxwell was traveling under British Passport No. 507441, and saw his occupation jotted down as "Copy Director" for a company known as Simpkin-Marshall with an address at Baker Street, London, England.

Maxwell had many aliases and changed what he said to people depending on his mood or need. His birth name was Jan Ludwig Hoch, but he used Ludwig Hoch, Captain Maxwell, Robert Maxwell, Ian Robert Maxwell, Wallace Chesteron and Enian Robert Maxwell interchangeably. After scribbling on his notepad, the inspector handed the passport back to the man with the bushy eyebrows.

Maxwell, accustomed to this line of questioning every time he arrived in the United States, thanked the inspector with a nod, placed his hat back on, slipped his passport back into his pocket, and quickly marched off into the crowd. Once he was out of sight the inspector disappeared into the back room and dialed a Washington, D.C. phone number. He supplied the FBI agent who answered with every detail exactly as it occurred and then went back to his station.

In addition to the paid informants at The Plaza, Hoover went one step further, installing two agents in a room adjacent to Maxwell's. He wanted to know every detail: whom Maxwell telephoned, what was said, where he went, who dropped by, who he had sex with and what type of sex was had. Hoover took pride in his attention to detail, and if that failed, he would achieve his desired result through deceit or lying. This is the trait that helped him rise through the ranks at the Department of Justice where the top men had as much disregard for the niceties of constitutional law as he did.

≈

J. Edgar Hoover and Robert Maxwell played cat and mouse for years. Internal FBI documents show it may have lasted throughout Hoover's life. Hoover was convinced Maxwell was a Soviet spy using his publishing empire to send intelligence behind the Iron Curtain.

Maxwell had begun to do business with scientific publishers while still a Captain for the British occupation authority called the Control Commission – a unit assigned to a section of the British Information Service. He was able to resolve red tape issues that restricted access to paper, marketing predicaments, and the safekeeping of inventories. Without any experience in publishing he proposed to German owned Springer-Verlag that they partner with him.

Springer's owners had concerns. While the occupation was temporary they did not know how long it would last. Maxwell, however, had demonstrated his ability to find resources and overcome obstacles. Germany was in ruins. Supplies and services were scarce or nonexistent. There weren't many avenues available and so Maxwell's offer was accepted. They let him set up a British firm so that he could market their publications outside of Germany.

Within one month Maxwell created a company in London naming it the European Publicity and Advertising Company, Ltd. Partnering with the Springer's again he formed another. This one Lange, Maxwell & Springer was used to market scientific publications worldwide.

His dreams of leaving his past entirely behind him and creating a brighter future were coming true.

Maxwell began to transfer via the military Springer's inventory – this at a time when non-military shipping was close to impossible. He also took on other publishers.

I discovered while researching that Robert Maxwell regularly made his wife, Betty, a partner in some of these companies – not all of which survived. Some were started and shuttered just as fast.

Germany had been the center of research in science, technology and medicine. Because of the war, German science journals were rare and worth their weight in gold.

Maxwell's brashness and boundless energy also attracted the attention of publishers James and Christopher Pitman. Pitman encouraged him to take over the ailing book wholesaler Simpkin Marshall. The company, whose warehouse was destroyed by bombs during the war, never properly recovered. And so, he simply added it to his growing empire.

Maxwell's publishing empire grew quickly and became his way to the riches he always dreamt of. In two years he had a staff of 120 people.

～

By the time of the liquidation proceedings for Simpkin Marshall, Ltd., the FBI noted inquiries had been made by people within the publishing industry. The allegations were that Maxwell was plundering the assets of the company. According to informants, "Maxwell is not considered to have a good business reputation, or to be a man of high integrity".

Unsecured creditors received pennies on the dollar after the bankruptcy. However, by the time the dust settled on the failed business, Maxwell owned the

British Book Center at 122 East 55th Street in midtown Manhattan in New York City. While there were complaints that he had purchased the valuable piece of real estate and the business with the liquidated company's money, there was yet no law on the books to hold him accountable for theft.

On the same lot sat the long-established Holliday bookshop owned by Robert Vanderbilt. Maxwell, now the landlord, told him to leave. He begrudgingly gave Vanderbilt a paltry $10,000 cash to leave the premises. The money was most likely part of the looted assets. Maxwell inherited high-end clientele, which included the Rockefellers, Kennedys, and the Jones' of Jones Beach.

Maxwell, who was only 32 at the time, was also strongly suspected of having unlawfully removed, or caused to be removed, from the company's premises confidential documents, including approximately 2,500 Adrema Addressing Machine plates, containing the names and addresses of export customers. He then used this information in another company he owned, I.R. Maxwell & Co. Ltd., which was a book exporting business.

Hoover's files on Maxwell became extensive. It no longer mattered whether Maxwell was in the United States or in the United Kingdom or anywhere in the world. Hoover had agents travel to wherever Maxwell was where they posed as potential business associates. These covert spies spoke with anyone associated with Maxwell or his wife.

Even the school where the couple's small children attended did not escape their scrutiny. Perhaps this is why Ghislaine, their youngest who was not yet born, was sent off to boarding school. The headmaster's wife, Mrs. Carr, was quite eager to gossip with the friendly FBI agents who queried her about Robert Maxwell.

"Mrs. Carr appeared to take the view that Maxwell gained by the company's liquidation and stated that Maxwell was connected with a number of other businesses and deals of a dubious nature. She stated Maxwell was a Czechoslovakian and was presumed to have changed his name by Deed Poll and not by naturalization. She stated that Maxwell's wife was of French nationality and was a likeable person of genuine character. She stated that although Maxwell appears to have a good character, his true character is not generally known as Maxwell confines himself to his own circle of business and personal associates.

Mrs. Carr further stated that Maxwell has not been known to give expression to any political views and takes no part in local affairs. She described Maxwell as being "very rich" and stated that he spent a good deal of time abroad, particularly in Russian and Iron Curtain countries. A number of foreign persons visit Maxwell at his address from time to time.

Mrs. Carr clearly distrusts and dislikes Maxwell and stated that she considered him to be an opportunist who had made a considerable amount of money from unknown sources. She stated that Maxwell's business and personal life were obscure."

A letter marked 'Secret' sent up the ranks to J. Edgar Hoover in February 1955 stated their investigation into Robert Maxwell found no evidence he had been working as a spy. An internal FBI note echoed the same—there was no evidence of espionage activity "on the part of Robert Maxwell in the United States; however ...". The rest of the sentence was redacted.

In 1958 Prescott Bush, father and grandfather to two U.S. Presidents, forwarded a letter to the FBI from Yale University. It stated their "concerns he may be engaged in a large-scale effort to transmit scientific information to the Russians".

While the FBI appeared to close their files on Robert Maxwell, history shows otherwise. This became evident over a decade after J. Edgar Hoover's death in 1972 which ended his tenure at the agency.

In their book, *Robert Maxwell, Israel's Superspy,* Gordon Thomas and Martin Dillon write:

"On a blistering hot day in January 1985, Robert Maxwell lumbered down the steps of his private Lear jet at Albuquerque airport. Behind him an aide carried the magnate's bulky briefcase, emblazoned with Maxwell's initials in gold leaf. This was the tycoon's second trip to Albuquerque in the past four months."

Maxwell presented himself to Sandia Laboratories – which is the core of U.S. nuclear weapons systems at Los Alamos – as the President of "Information on Demand" (IOD). IOD maintained an office in San Francisco near the home of Maxwell's daughter Isabel and her husband, Dale Djerassi.

In 1982 he purchased it through Pergamon Press from its owner Sue Rugge, a former librarian. The company became a front for Mossad. It was the same year Maxwell was recruited by Israeli spymaster Rafi Eitan to sell compromised versions of PROMIS software with a Signal Intelligence (SIGINT) "back-door" enabling them to spy. Eitan was known for traveling with his 14-year-old sex-slave he'd acquired from a Latin American country and for his partnership with Fidel Castro in Cuba.

FBI documents reveal that employees of Sandia National Laboratories were concerned about Robert Maxwell and IOD's access to the U.S. government's nuclear databases.

The FBI did nothing.

To date, portions of their investigation into Robert Maxwell's dealings with Sandia National Laboratories at Los Alamos remain classified.

FIVE

Betty Maxwell

———————————

While much has been written about Robert Maxwell, his wife, Elisabeth, remains safely tucked away in his shadow. Known as Betty, she was born Elisabeth Jenny Jeanne Meynard in La Grive, near Saint-Alban-de-Roche, France on March 11, 1921. Her parents were Louis Paul Meynard and Colombe (nee Petel) Meynard. Paul, as he was known, was a Protestant descendant of the Huguenot upper class. He owned a silk-weaving factory and was the mayor of the tiny village. Colombe was a Roman Catholic and was promptly excommunicated for having married a Protestant.

At the time of Betty's birth Saint-Alban-de-Roche had a population of approximately 800 people. Her hometown, La Grive, was significantly smaller. It was Betty's ancestors, who in the early 1800s, drained the marshes of the River Bourbre (a tributary of the Rhône River) in order to build fabric mills.

In need for workers, the Meynard family brought in Italian laborers. Many Italians who emigrated were illiterate and could only earn their livelihood through manual labor. To provide their new labor force with a roof over their heads, they had approximately one hundred homes assembled—presumably by the same laborers. A school and an infirmary were added—which Betty Maxwell claims in her memoir was "unheard of" in those days. The mill was a sweatshop where men, women and children worked long hours to be paid a pittance. Factory work, by its very nature, is oppression and toil for the masses with the riches and wealth going to the very few. It's a microcosm of wealth inequality—the haves and have-nots. Betty was the former, having been born into a life of privilege. The weaving factory was the sole source of work and, therefore, income for the residents in La Grive—making it impossible for them to negotiate either hours or pay. One either worked for them, or if they decided not to, had to move elsewhere.

Of note, weaving families in France and England were primarily of Huguenot descent—where sons apprenticed with their fathers. These men usually became wealthy and had a keen sense of business. The production of silk was interconnected with many other trades—including fashion designers. These early designers were known as dressmakers or couturières who toiled for weeks creating the luxurious and intricate clothing worn by the upper classes, aristocracy and the royals.

Betty's father, Paul, was 45 at the time of her birth. He was a descendant from the kings of France through Robert d'Anjou. He was also known as Robert the Wise, King of Naples, titular King of Jerusalem, Count of Provence and Forcalquier from 1309 to 1343. Upon his father's accession to the throne in 1309, he became the Duke of Calabria. All records showing her family tree mysteriously disappeared off the internet after Jeffrey Epstein's death in 2019.

In her biography, Betty describes her father as "a handsome man, renowned for his charm and exceptional gifts as a raconteur." She claims that she and her sister, Yvonne, whom the family called Vonnie, heard tales of his affairs with some of the well-known ladies of the Belle Epoque. Among these Mata Hari, the exotic dancer and alleged spy, who Betty states wrote love letters to her father using her married name, Mrs. McLeod, as a clever way to disguise her identity.

Betty's mother, Colombe, was eight years younger than her dashing and naughty husband. On the surface, they appear to be polar opposites. She was neither wealthy or beautiful. Her saving grace was that she was charming, dressed elegantly and was courageous. Despite the "courageous" attribute, Betty describes her as a frail homebody prone to constant migraines.

During World War I, Colombe was a telephone supervisor who passed on information about enemy positions to army headquarters—risking her life had she been caught. This is the very definition of a spy and it brings up the question: is spying the family business on both sides of Ghislaine Maxwell's family tree?

Adolph Hitler and Vichy France

Many years later, during World War II, Colombe was reinstated in the Telephone Service on a senior level at the request of Henri Philippe Benoni Omer Petain. It was he who decorated her for her bravery during the first world war. Petain was a French general officer who, by the end of World War I, had risen up to the position of Marshal of France. At the ripe old age of 80, in 1940, he served as Chief of State of Vichy France until 1948.

In the days before cell phones and computers, the civilian telephone system was used as a surveillance tool. Wiretapping, like the interception of mail, was one of the ways governments committed espionage against their citizens. This goes back to when America was still a colony—when the King's mandate sanctioned the government's ability to intercept all mail within the British Empire. In post-revolutionary France, Joseph Fouché, the statesman and Minister of Police, intercepted mail for Napoleon Bonaparte. During World War II, in occupied France, these tactics were used to help the Nazis—not the Resistance.

In July 1940 the German tanks rolled into France splitting it into two regions. One was occupied by Hitler's soldiers, and the other—about 200 miles southeast of Paris—was run by a puppet regime led by General Philippe Petain. Petain was a notorious antisemite and implemented harsher treatment than the Germans. He was responsible for deporting Jews to the Nazi concentration camps and for relentlessly torturing the prisoners—those who were Jewish as well as members of the Resistance. In Paul Baudouin's 1946 book, *The Private Diaries of Paul Baudouin* he wrote that it was Petain who argued for harsher policies actions against Jews, and not his prime minister, Pierre Laval, as was thought at the time. On October 15, 1945 Laval was found guilty of treason and was executed—after attempting the cowardly act of trying to poison himself.

This history of collaboration in France is fascinating and little known. France had traitors who collaborated with the Nazi regime—and Betty Maxwell's parents were among these. The myth of the Resistance put forth by Charles de Gaulle is a lie. On June 18, 1940 he made an appeal via BBC radio, urging his countrymen to continue to resist the Germans. His famous words, "Whatever happens, the flame of the French resistance must not and will not be extinguished." De Gaulle was far removed—as he was in England—and what he

85

wanted was for people to forget the harsh reality of the war. By this time, the government of France had formally surrendered to Hitler.

Petain was tried for treason at the end of the war. He had signed extreme antisemitic ordinances against Jews under Hitler's occupation of France. After the trial, which took place from July 23 to August 15, 1945, he was convicted on all charges and sentenced to death. Charles de Gaulle commuted the sentence to life imprisonment due to his advanced age and his military contributions during World War I.

Among the people who appealed for Petain's release were Queen Mary, Edward VIII—the Duke of Windsor (who abdicated the throne to marry the twice divorced American Wallis Simpson), and President Harry S. Truman (who sanctioned Operation Paperclip). Operation Paperclip was a covert intelligence program in which more than 1,600 German Nazi scientists, engineers and others were moved out of Nazi Germany to the United States. Some of whom were given top positions in NASA and in Ivy League universities.

≈

In her role as a wife, Colombe dedicated herself to preserving the outdated traditions of Paul's aristocratic background. Like her mother before her, Betty would also dedicate herself to her husband's needs. The most visible was bearing nine children—an act meant to replace the family he lost in the Nazi concentration camps.

While researching Betty's parents I found myself imagining Paul as a man who never tired of telling anyone within earshot of his prestigious pedigree. In this way, he reminded me of Robert Maxwell. Both men are similar in character by overstating their own importance to the point of ridicule.

A 1917 photo of Betty's father show a balding man with a roundish face and a jutting chin. He sports a full toothbrush mustache, which was fashionable in the early 20th century, and was later adopted by Adolph Hitler. While not the handsome man this author expected to see after reading Betty Maxwell's description of him—it is not uncommon for a daughter to find her father more attractive than he actually is. Betty inherited his large protruding nose and unfortunate upside down L-shaped chin. Photos of her tend to be front-facing, but I managed to find at some where she is in profile. Her chin detracts from the rest of her features which are somewhat appealing. Ghislaine Maxwell has a similar profile, but to a lesser degree.

Betty and Vonnie attended the local school for children. Betty was five and had already learned how to read by the time she was four. The two sisters were placed at the very front and were separated by a wide space between them and the rest of the children. This was done to prevent them from catching lice.

Betty Maxwell's education

In 1930, at the age of 9, she was sent to England to attend the convent of Our Lady of Compassion at Acocks Green in Birmingham. Two years later, at age 11, she returned to France.

By the time she was 15, Betty took no interest in her school work and instead of going straight home spent her time strolling up and down the Rue de La Republique—Lyon's main street—pressing her nose against the windows of the fashionable stores and treating herself to caramels made by street vendors. Her parents, bewildered by her behavior, packed her off to live with her godmother whom Betty called Aunt Jeanne in Saint Omer. Upon her arrival, she was placed in the local high school—which was essentially a school for boys.

The Devil and apparitions

Fernand, a cousin of hers, the youngest son of her mother's eldest brother, who was a priest and died young in a strange drowning accident off the coast of Bilbao is the person, Betty claims, who changed her opinion about the existence of the Devil. They would often go to the National Gallery to view the early Flemish paintings. He always took the time to explain the intricate details and revelatory symbols to her.

In her memoir she writes:

"One day, he had been examining a particular Virgin and Child for ages and I was getting tired, so I sat down on one of the narrow benchlike settees which were then situated in the middle of the long galleries. As soon as I sat down, an extremely unpleasant man, dressed all in black, rather weird-looking and disquieting, came to sit beside me. I remember feeling so uncomfortable and so cold all of a sudden that I got up and walked the few paces which separated me from my cousin, who was still lost in contemplation of the picture.

'I'm joining you because I'm frightened of the man sitting next to me,' I said. But when we both turned to look at him, there was no one there; no sign of him. I just could not believe my eyes! We had a good view of the entire length of the gallery in both directions and there was nobody who fitted my description. I felt so ill at ease and embarrassed as I tried to explain that there really had been someone there. I was sure that Fernand

would think I was mistaken and make fun of me. On the contrary, with immense composure he said, 'Don't worry. It's the Devil, he's always pestering me, take no notice.'

Betty Maxwell was never able to erase the memory of that day and from that moment on experienced similar encounters.

The Sorbonne

At the age of 18, in 1939 as World War I broke out, Betty began her studies at the Sorbonne. Established in the 13th century, it is one of the oldest and most prestigious universities in the world. During the war the male student population shrunk as many joined the armed services and lost their lives. This had no impact on the male instructors as they were considered too old to enlist. At one point female students made up over 40% of the total population.

Among the courses she took was the Cordon Blue cooking class. It was a class also attended by Parisian hostesses and society women who wanted to improve their skills. Betty does not appear to have had a passion for any role. She began her studies at the Sorbonne with the idea of getting a degree in philosophy, however, when her father took up studying the law, he persuaded her to do the same because it was much more practical.

The wife of Robert Maxwell

Betty is usually described as the "long-suffering, loyal and innocent wife" of ruthless crook Maxwell. However, that may not be an accurate description of the woman he considered his equal.

While still using the alias Leslie Du Maurier, he proposed marriage during their first lunch. This is something men with an agenda, not based on love, appear to do. Before becoming "Robert Maxwell" he secured himself a wife who could guarantee his entrance into the world of high society. And, to top it off, she was a descendant of French kings. Throughout his life he never tired of having himself photographed with members of the United Kingdom's Royal Family. These photos were prominently displayed in his offices and throughout his home.

It was the French-born Betty's good manners and refinement that helped the ruffian Maxwell pass himself off socially. She constantly reminded him that "manners maketh man" even though, as the years flew by, he became less and less concerned of how he appeared to anyone.

Betty was a virgin when they shared their first sexual encounter. Of that memorable event she writes:

"Although he was ablaze with desire, he did not rush me. I was ready for love, eager to be at one with him ... But despite my readiness, it was a painful first experience. He was in tears at the thought of having hurt me. Nothing was ever to move me more than my husband's tears."

She complained that every time he looked at her she got pregnant. Her sister, Vonnie, who became a gynecologist, delivered all her children in Maisons-Laffitte, France. The couple would eventually have nine children – two died early.

An interesting insight into their marriage can be gleaned from their behavior when their eldest son, Michael, went into a coma after an accident.

During the eight years that Michael remained a vegetable at the hospital, Betty believed she was the only one to visit him. Her husband never accompanied her. However, at some point after Michael succumbed and died, she learned he did visit their son. Maxwell would leave the house and instruct their driver to stop by the hospital where he would sit by his firstborn son's bedside for hours. Why he never shared this with his wife may be interpreted as him not wanting to show signs of weakness—especially to her. Having a 'stiff upper lip' is a particularly English trait. It was not socially acceptable to show one's feelings when distraught. The origins of this concept go back to the Spartans in Ancient Greece—who believed in stoicism, discipline and self-sacrifice. The writer Edward Morgan Forster famously bemoaned his fellow Englishmen as having "well-developed bodies, fairly developed minds and undeveloped hearts".

In her memoir, Betty pretends to gives us a glimpse into her private life with her ever-demanding husband. The book, frankly, has less to do with her life than it is a tribute to Maxwell—who ironically she was ready to divorce just before his death. It is also, in this writer's opinion, Betty's opportunity to re-write history about her husband not being a spy. And, more importantly, underscoring what she repeatedly told the press after

Maxwell died. She knew nothing about the multiple financial frauds.

Her blithe passages where she doesn't even condone her parents for their obvious antisemitism literally left me stunned. This is an example of gaslighting in its finest. On the other hand, Betty's memoir would have been a wonderful story if she had written about making the best of an unhappy marriage and her struggle to become known for her own accomplishments. However, this does not appear to be the reason it was written.

This author does not believe Betty Maxwell did not know what her husband was up to. She knew about the other women. She knew when he was lying. She knew about it all. Denial doesn't change facts. From their earliest days together, he added her as a partner in enterprises that were clearly bankruptcy scams. What Betty does, on occasion, is launch into a sermon bemoaning the decline of her marriage and the abuse she tolerated in order to elicit sympathy from both her family and the reader.

For example, she writes, "He would constantly revert to the same old theme—that I did not look after his material needs to a standard he considered acceptable and was therefore incapable of ensuring his happiness. Sometimes there would be a button missing on a shirt, or I would forget his evening shirt studs or black tie when I packed his bag. He would complain that his cupboards were not impeccably tidy or that I hadn't got his summer clothes out early enough ... What he wanted me to do was assist, bolster and serve him and the children."

The letters from him reinforce his expectation of her as his wife.

"Betuska my love,

You most certainly have made big strides towards becoming the perfect partner though the things you have done like washing my clothes, or darning my socks ... Although by themselves they may seem trivial and matter-of-fact, do not be deceived by that because they constitute the demonstration of the love we have for each other, and to me they are of the highest value, for without them our love could not live."

Her letters to him show she is willing to do anything he asks. Some are difficult to read because she is groveling for his attention and already fleeing affection:

"I want to live for you, I want to drown my soul in your desires. This requires all my attention and all my strength, there is no time to do anything else. You will

only need to say what you want and it will be done, or to express a desire and I will satisfy it. Perhaps you will discover that the half-flayed creature you have stripped naked still deserves to be loved."

Out of their nine children—seven survived—which kept Betty busy while her husband pressed on with his life. When he needed her to campaign with him during his Parliamentary period in the 1960s, she dutifully packed the children off to their grandparents in France. They remained there for six long months during which she devoted all her time to his effort. In 1964 representing the Labour Party, Maxwell was elected as Member of Parliament (MP) for Buckingham and re-elected in 1966. He served until 1970.

The fact that Robert Maxwell was Jewish was not a problem for anyone except for Betty. It gnawed on her that he'd married outside of his faith. This, despite the fact that Robert Maxwell married her because she wasn't Jewish. For many years he followed the advice his mother had given to him in his young teens: "To behave and act like an Englishman is to be successful." Maxwell was also a social climber and it's likely Betty snagged herself a husband by simply proclaiming she was a descendant of French Kings. The sex-addicted braggart, whose physique grew larger with each passing year, could not have been what the virginal Betty planned when she agreed to marry a man whose name wasn't really his and who hid behind his movie star good looks while pretending to be a gentleman.

Betty, the hostess

Betty Maxwell thoroughly enjoyed being the wife of a tycoon and everything it afforded her. The clothing, the travel, the entertaining. She reveled in the praise bestowed upon her as a hostess, "People tell me that my dining room was rather like one of those celebrated Parisian salons." She prided herself in receiving London's upper class and politicians into their grand estate.

Gyles Brandreth, an English writer and politician, was a guest at one of their parties in the 1970s. Nothing struck him out of the ordinary at first. "It was only when I went up to Maxwell that I realized he had this apparatus on. There was an old-fashioned microphone attached to the lapel of his jacket with a windshield on it. And on his belt was this large box, the size of a hardback book with a dial in the middle. This was somehow connected to speakers in each of the rooms." Brandreth realized that Maxwell was wearing his personal PA system. It enabled him to address people from anywhere. "He'd turn the dial down when he was talking to you. Then, as soon as he saw someone he wanted to talk to on the other side of the room, he'd turn it up again, and this disembodied voice would come booming out of the speakers."

Betty ran Headington Hill Hall like a hotel for his business interests which is similar to how Ghislaine Maxwell ran Jeffrey Epstein's homes. She kept hundreds of scrap books with her husband's press cuttings. And for his birthday, every year, they had grand parties. Captains of industry and the social set descended upon their house on the hill to enjoy the opulent and pompous extravaganzas.

Peter Mandelson, a British Labor politician, was among the many people who attended their parties. "It's very strange because you'd simultaneously want to be at Maxwell's parties and at the same time shrink away from him," he said. "Because he was such a bully and so unpredictable. To be honest, I was frightened of his company. He had that ability to make you feel completely small and inadequate, and that just scrambled my head."

The other women

During their entire married life, Betty ignored the revolving door of women that ended up in his bed while he ignored her completely.

When she discovered he was having an affair with his young personal assistant she comforts herself with her own faithfulness. In her book she writes, "Nor could I understand how a girl would allow herself to fall in love with the father of six children under the age of eight, whatever the circumstances. It was not the kind of moral code I had been brought up on, and I can say in all honesty that I have never allowed myself to fall in love with a married man."

According to the book *Robert Maxwell, Israel's Superspy* one of Maxwell's lovers was an MI6 spy. She labeled him a sexual predator adding, "He had those eyes which would undress me from across a crowded room. Once he had me through the bedroom door, he was all over me. The result was he usually came to orgasm during our foreplay. But he was always very generous in his gifts. He gave me expensive jewelry at Christmas and on my birthday. Only after our affair had ended did I discover he had given other women the same gifts. After he had sex, he was gone in minutes. Looking back, he regarded a woman as little more than someone to satisfy his physical demands. He would often call me at all hours to come to the penthouse."

Was Betty truly the martyr she painted herself to be in her one-sided marriage to Robert Maxwell or had she become too accustomed to the chauffeur-driven Rolls Royce, exotic trips, and life of privilege to leave?

Maxwell often said, "I can't get along with men. I tried having male assistants at first, but it didn't work. They tend to be too independent. Men like to have individuality. Women can become an extension of the boss."

Throughout her description of their marriage, one cannot miss the sensual tension between the dominant partner, Bob, and the submissive Betty. Of her having to do things in a certain way to please him. Of him telling her it wasn't good enough. And, the sting she felt on her checks with every reprimand.

Their marriage seems like a prequel to the erotic romance novel *Fifty Shades of Grey* by British author E.L. James published in 2011—many years after their life together was over.

Beating of the children

The mental abuse and punishment was not restricted to Betty. It seeped into the next generation. Their children were an extension of themselves and as such, they too, were subjected to beatings when they misbehaved.

She wrote in her book after his death, "Bob would threaten and rant at the children until they were reduced to pulp." The Times in London reported, "At mealtimes in Oxford, Maxwell questioned his children about world affairs. In the event of a mistake, the meal was interrupted while Maxwell physically beat the child in front of the others. If a comment in a school report was not perfect, Maxwell caned the child. If the meal was brief, he would make one child the scapegoat of his anger."

Although Betty claimed in her book that she might have "gone too far" when he "persecuted his children, as he did every Sunday, reducing them to tears, each in turn, week by week" – she claims it was important for her to maintain a unified front before the children.

At one time, when Ian was 15 she gave him the option of waiting for his father to come home or getting "disciplined" by her. She writes, "After a moment of reflection, he decided to take the beating from me...I hated doing it and needed all the courage I could muster to perform such a hated punishment with the twins' riding crop."

Only Ghislaine, many said, escaped the full wrath Robert Maxwell's twisted perversion.

After 20 years of marriage, Robert took Betty to Africa on a safari. She thought it would be a romantic holiday for the two of them until her husband, anxious to be back in his world, returned to London leaving her alone.

She wrote to him the next day:

"For some years now, I have realized, at first with bellicose sadness, then with hurt pride and at last with victorious serenity, that my usefulness to you has come to an end...As a supreme act of my love for you, I will make no more demands on your physical and mental love and I relieve you as of now of any sense of guilt that might creep in."

Betty could not have been unaware of the fact that since the beginning of their marriage, her husband had been having one affair after the other. While he might have been more discreet in the beginning of their marriage he became less so as one child after the other was born.

Nor could the refined Betty claim to be oblivious to his ill manners and crudeness.

Robert Maxwell regularly soiled his silk bed sheets at night, shit with the door open, never flushed the toilet and used flannel towels to wipe leaving them strewn on the floor. He let his Filipino maids, Julia and Elsa, take care of the soiled towels and sheets without a thought as to how utterly disgusting it was for another human to wash off his excrement.

He was also known to drop the silver trays where his meals were delivered to him by his butler on the floor if the food was cold or if he'd changed his mind and wanted to eat something else. The butlers would pick up the discarded food quietly so as not to disturb him. Maxwell also fired people at whim. Just before Christmas one year he fired an employee after accusing him of stealing fifty cents. And one time, Ian, his son was late to a meeting and he, too, was fired. Psychiatrists would later say Robert Maxwell most likely suffered from bipolar mental disorder.

Neil Kinnock, a member of the Labour Party, said of him, "I was in this constant dilemma of not wanting to lose his support. How do you deal with this extremely capricious man with an overwhelming sense of his own power? While I knew I couldn't afford to lose his support I knew too that he could change in an instance; it was like walking on eggshells."

In 1984 after Robert Maxwell purchased *The Mirror* Kinnock and his wife invited the Maxwells to an informal dinner at their local Italian restaurant. They were astonished to see Maxwell and Betty arrive in separate Rolls-Royces, walk in and pretend all was normal. Fact is—it *was* normal for them.

Semion Mogilevich | Samuel Pisar

In 1988 when Robert Maxwell was obtaining an Israeli passport for Semion Mogilevich along with another 23 for his associates, Betty introduced him to Samuel Pisar.

"I had originally introduced Sam to Bob after the unforgettable impression he made on me when I went to ask him to address a conference I was chairing on the Holocaust in 1988. His famous book, "Of Blood and Hope, in which he relates his experiences as a youngster in a Nazi death camp, had touched me profoundly."

In the 1980s Maxwell was helping to launder money for the Mossad. Mogilevich, at this time, was stealing from Jewish refugees who were emigrating to Israel and the United States from the Soviet Union. Pretending to help them by buying their assets, telling them he would sell these at market value and then send them the proceeds after they were settled—he kept the money. In Craig Unger's book, *American Kompromat,* he writes: "Maxwell became a bagman of sorts who moved millions of dollars around at the toss of a hat. He became very close to the Politburo. The information he provided was priceless. He began sharing valuable

Western technology with Moscow—stealing it, really—and worked every side of the fence, spending one day in the White House with Reagan, the next in the Kremlin, and then, perhaps off to Israel."

At precisely the same time that Maxwell is helping Mogilevich fleece Jewish refugees, Betty has established herself as an expert on the Holocaust. She even organizes a conference called "Remembering for the Future." When writing about who helped her in the aftermath of Maxwell's death, she states:

"The arrival of Sam and Judith Pisar was a great solace. I had originally introduced Sam to Bob after the unforgettable impression he made on me when I went to ask him to address a conference I was chairing on the Holocaust in 1988. His famous book, Of Blood and Hope, in which he relates his experience as a youngster in a Nazi death camp, had also touched me profoundly. I remember returning from Paris and saying to Bob that I had just met a man who had made the strongest impression on me since I met him, Bob, all those years ago. I also remember his answer: Then I must meet that man too."

Anyone who has examined the Maxwell family would be naïve not to wonder if Betty Maxwell's work on the Holocaust was the equivalent of Ghislaine

Maxwell's TerraMar non-profit. Non-profits and philanthropic work go hand in hand with not only the fleecing of the public but are also used to create a false public front.

The intentional buffoon?

As the years flew by Robert Maxwell became massively overweight, breathing garlic from the folds of his body. And when he spoke he was either shouting or cursing. Despite this, he continued to seduce women, was hugely charismatic and many of the people who worked with him were fiercely loyal.

As the Parisian daughter of an upper-class family Betty had to be aware of his boorish behavior in public. The once poor orphan had become one of Britain's richest and most grandiose characters. His ego had become so monstrous that he was ridiculed behind his back. Even Queen Elizabeth had a laugh at his expense naming her spaniel dog after him.

Robert Maxwell bounded up the steps of the stage as the ballerina performed for London's high society at a charity function. The grotesquely obese man interrupted her and began to demonstrate the proper way she should move. The audience whispered amongst themselves things they would not dare say to Maxwell's face.

Everyone who knew him had an opinion.

And those who worked for him feared him.

No one was neutral about *Captain Bob*. Anyone who came into contact with him or observed him shared their disdain for his overbearing manner.

Even strangers.

Betty Maxwell appears to have been the only person who neither feared him nor hated him. Perhaps in her eyes he remained the young handsome soldier she met in Paris after the war. What she had to know with certainty was his belief that one was born either as a master or slave.

Years later, they stopped sharing a bedroom and both began to think about not just a separation but a divorce.

Robert Maxwell began to spend more time at an apartment he kept in London behaving as if he were a bachelor. He'd gorge on Chinese food, urinate off rooftops and appeared to be quite tired of family life.

1990

In July 1990 he told Betty he wanted a "legal separation and that it had to be advertised in the *Times*." It wasn't. "I don't want to see you again, I don't want you to phone me, I don't want to talk to you anymore. I no longer love you."

Robert Maxwell's indifference to his wife was also observed by others. Nick Davies, who worked with Maxwell as his foreign editor on the *Daily Mirror* said, "He treated her quite disgracefully – he would be rude to her in front of people, say at official dinners. When she fussed over him, Maxwell would not hesitate to tell her to 'fuck off'."

Divorce was also on Betty's mind. It was just a matter of how to approach him and ask for one that would be suitable for her. Before either one of the two could take a step into finalizing their marriage, Robert Maxwell drowned at sea on November 5, 1991.

It is worth noting that Jeffrey Epstein was considered a person of interest in the death of Robert Maxwell.

SIX

Purgatory Press

───────────

The operating room was full of unfamiliar technical equipment. On the surgical table lay a slight blonde woman about to undergo electro shock therapy. A tall dark-haired man dressed in a suit pushes open the door. The doctors ask him to leave. "I will not leave!" Robert Maxwell declares as he lifts the woman off the table and into his arms. This is how Eleanor Berry, daughter of Lord Michael Harwell, remembers Maxwell.

In her book *My Unique Relationship with Robert Maxwell,* she credits him for saving her life when he "charged into an operating theatre" where she was receiving electro-convulsive therapy, scooped her up, and carried her to his car.

Aside from her curious lifelong fixation with the boisterous Maxwell, Ms. Berry now in her late 70s, boasts via her website, that she once compiled an unpublished contextual thesis on the *Marquis de Sade*.

Sade was famous for what was referred to as his *libertine sexuality,* meaning he was devoid of moral principles, a normal sense of responsibility, and sexual restraint. He believed in sexual cruelty and wrote about this in his erotic works depicting sexual fantasies with an emphasis on violence, suffering, anal sex and crime.

Not surprisingly, Jeffrey Epstein, who years into the future would become Ghislaine Maxwell's chosen partner, lived his life in the style of Sade. He provided visitors a glimpse into his dark world by displaying copies of the Marquis de Sade's *The Misfortunes of Virtue* intentionally left on tables throughout his various homes. It was a clear act of thumbing his nose at the world. Epstein, like Ghislaine's father, clearly believed the rules did not apply to him.

It's an obscene book—one which prompted Napoleon to order Sade jailed. It's about a 12-year-old French girl named Justine who travels alone through the country and ends up in a monastery where she is forced to become the sex slave of monks and where she endures repeated sexual assaults and is ordered to participate in orgies. This is eerily similar to the horrors described by the victims of Epstein and Maxwell.

Decades before the saga of Epstein and Maxwell came to public attention, Berry claims that Robert Maxwell became a surrogate father to her. While she maintains it was a platonic relationship, there are indications that her feelings for him were exactly the opposite. She lusted for him.

Her father, Michael Berry, later known as Lord Hartwell, owned the *Daily Telegraph* and the *Sunday Telegraph* – rivals of the Maxwell owned *Mirror*. One would have to wonder what Robert Maxwell's true intentions were when he befriended Eleanor Berry. Was Maxwell collecting information on his rival by keeping the man's daughter nearby? It's certainly plausible. He certainly wasn't the sort of man who did anyone any favors.

In many ways Eleanor viewed Maxwell in the same manner as Ghislaine—she adored him. Berry flirted openly with him and compared him to a "beautiful, big black bear".

According to Berry, on Christmas in 1970, when Ghislaine turned nine, her parents gave her a pony. "She loved horses at this time," Berry begins, "as she had yet to discover boys and men. Her doting attention to them posed no threat to her father who, as she grew up, would become profoundly jealous of her many boyfriends."

One morning while Eleanor and Bob, as she refers to him, were walking around the grounds of Headington Hill Hall they noticed someone left the gate of the tennis court open. Ghislaine's pony had wandered onto the court leaving mounds of dunk everywhere. It had also eaten its way through the net. The nine-year-old was lying on the grass outside the tennis court with her legs bent playing 'God Save the Queen' on a recorder.

"What is the pony doing on the tennis court?" Robert howled.

Eleanor began laughing and Maxwell's anger subsided. In a more controlled tone he continued, "It's not so much that I mind your pony being on the tennis court. But, I won't tolerate his leaving his visiting card behind."

A startled Ghislaine sat up while her father marched off to into the office of Pergamon Press leaving Eleanor behind with Ghislaine.

"I'm due to receive a hiding from my father," the little girl said cheekily.

Eleanor writes that she managed to bite off the words "Lucky old you," and instead asked her what she did to annoy him.

"I asked Judy and Jean to do some extra work for me."

"Who are Judy and Jean and what did you ask them to do?"

"They are secretaries I told them to organize the transport of some horses. I asked these women to arrange to bring the horses back to Oxford."

"Did your father say it was alright?"

"No."

"What sort of hiding is your father going to give you?"

"Come into the house and I will show you. Daddy always allows me to choose what he beats me with." Ghislaine pushed herself off the grass and grabbed Eleanor by the hand. She then marched straight into the house and led her into one of its many rooms. Inside the room was a table and Ghislaine pointed to it. On the table were displayed an array of different objects.

"Which one will you choose?" Eleanor calmly inquired.

"The shoe horn doesn't hurt," Ghislaine said matter-of-factly.

"Does your father beat you with your trousers on or off?"

"On."

Eleanor writes that she was disappointed to hear this but kept the thought to herself.

"I'll tell daddy to use the shoehorn. It doesn't hurt."

And then Ghislaine asked, "Which one would you choose, Eleanor, if my father wanted to beat you?"

"Well Ghislaine I personally would choose the cane. The one that makes the swooshing noise in the air. Oh, sorry I didn't mean to give you any funny ideas. Forget what I said."

The child looked puzzled and Berry wondered if she had completely lost her mind.

"I would ask your father to let you take your trousers off. Then I would ask him to beat me with the cane," Eleanor added, enunciating every word.

"What on your bare bottom?" Ghislaine queried puzzled by what she'd heard.

"Why yes," Eleanor replied. In her book, Berry claims she didn't have her wits about her because she had caught some sun while walking with Bob earlier. Apparently, sun rays appear to have been enough to whip her into a sexual frenzy so that she was consumed with the fantasy of Robert Maxwell using the cane to lash her naked buttocks.

"Why would you ask my father to beat you on your bare bottom with the cane particularly when the cane is the most painful of the lot? What you're saying doesn't make sense."

Eleanor Berry realized she had said too much. Enough for Ghislaine to possibly tell her father. She became fearful and somewhat ashamed for having given in to conversing like this with the child.

"Tell me the truth, Eleanor, would you really like to be beaten on your bare bottom by my father?"

The words "Oh Christ, yes" were struggling to be released from her lips, she wrote in her book, but added that she managed to control herself.

"I did the most dreadful things when I was your age and no one whipped me."

Eleanor Berry would go on to forge a long-lived relationship with some of Maxwell's children. Ian and Kevin more so than the others. She also wrote several books on Robert Maxwell.

The spanking incident Eleanor Berry references happened in the summer of 1970. Several weeks later Ghislaine Maxwell, age 9, was sent off to Edgarley Hall boarding school located in Somerset. One hundred miles away from her precious Headington Hill Hall, her pony and her servants.

The Victorian architecture of the school looks like a scene out of Harry Potter. There were porches and caves and grottoes spread across the green expanse. What had once been a boys-only school opened their doors to girls during the 1960s.

By the time the 9-year-old dawdled through the grand entrance and stood in the foyer with the high ceilings and walls adorned with paintings of times long gone, the school had earned a reputation for dealing successfully with dyslexic students. Perhaps here her parents surely believed Ghislaine would get the help she needed for her disability.

Her father had gotten into the habit of inviting children to Headington Hill Hall which had become known as the "Versailles on the Hill above Oxford" to take part in reading competitions with his youngest.

What should be noted is that it wasn't Ghislaine who invited the girls—but her father. He didn't play fair even here because while some of the other girls were better and clearly should have won—he always declared Ghislaine the winner. It's clear he did this to bolster the confidence that she, in all likelihood, lacked. She would, in short order overcome this. However, at the time, his daughter was the exact opposite of his beloved mother. For his youngest child there were going to be obstacles—he would have to do his best to prepare her for a good marriage. One to a suitable and wealthy aristocrat worthy of her love.

To that end, the otherwise penny-pinching Robert Maxwell spent money ensuring she was welcome everywhere. When birthday parties were held for Ghislaine, her school friends left with piles of expensive gifts. She had become somewhat of a bully as she defended against the hurtful taunts by the other children because of her inability to read as well as they did.

What she lacked in reading she made up for in sports – which she excelled in. Jostling about with the other students also improved her social skills tremendously.

Children of the elite, however, do not always turn out well when they are cared for by the help and sent off to be looked after by strangers at prep schools. It's now referred to as "privileged abandonment". There's palpable damage done to minors who experience trauma when separating from their parents. Many people who have spent their childhoods in boarding school tend to shut down emotionally and freeze out when faced with something that is sad or frightening or infuriating. Psychological studies show that people who were sent off to boarding school in their childhoods do not experience empathy. They believe that experiencing hardship is actually a good thing.

None of the Maxwell children had large groups of friends. For their birthday parties other children—not their friends—were invited to supplement the number of youngsters at these events.

Betty Maxwell loved to collect photos which she dutifully put into numerous albums. This habit of creating a fictional front is one Ghislaine will also embrace.

While no one knows what it must have been like to grow up under the cloud of darkness that was Robert Maxwell – it could not have been easy. Except for Ghislaine – who has been repeatedly reported as being his "cherished child". It was her lone photograph that he displayed in his penthouse office. And, in return for his doting attention, she adored him.

Even at 9 years of age Ghislaine hated any woman, aside from her mother, who was the object of her father's attention. The first woman to be subjected to her wrath and envy was Jean Baddeley. Baddeley was her father's personal assistant of 20 years who shared almost every working moment with him. She was also his faithful traveling companion as he trotted across the globe.

Jean Baddeley's name was found in Jeffrey Epstein's black book.

Ghislaine, Kevin and Ian—the three youngest of the family—were born within five years of each other. Kevin is one year older than his sister and Ian four years older. The three of them often talked about how much they despised Jean. Even Betty Maxwell was aware her husband was, in all likelihood, having an affair with her. Baddeley, however, lasted longer than any of his other assistants spending 20 years at his side.

Pretty, blonde, thin with a ready smile and smart clothes young Ghislaine loathed her for years.

Upon his death, Robert Maxwell left Jean a £100,000 inheritance. She also owned several companies set up at the request of Robert Maxwell, one of these employed Kevin Maxwell after his unexpected death.

～

At 13, after spending four years at Edgarley, now known as Millfield Preparatory School, Ghislaine went on to Headington Girls' School at Oxford – another boarding school – where she excelled at playing tennis, hockey and athletics in general.

Ben Macintrye, a historian, author and newspaper columnist, has a sister who was one of Ghislaine's schoolmates. He quoted her as saying Ghislaine was "an unlikely figure of glamour among the dons' daughters' who attended the prestigious Oxford school." And added, "Ghislaine was envied, admired, teased for her money, and mocked for her slow reading."

During my research I discovered Ghislaine suffered from dyslexia. Which wasn't well understood in those days and not disclosed by any of the Maxwells to anyone outside of the family.

A well-known alumna of Headington Girls' School at Oxford was Christina Onassis – 11 years older than Ghislaine and daughter of billionaire shipping tycoon Aristotle "Ari" Onassis.

Five years after the assassination of her husband, President John F. Kennedy, Jacqueline "Jackie" Kennedy married Onassis on October 20, 1968. Onassis was 23 years her senior and one headline read, *Jackie Marries a Blank Check*. Christina, spoiled rotten by her wealthy flamboyant father, hated Jackie. She and her brother Alexander referred to the former first lady as *The Gold-digger*. Until her father's marriage she had been the focus of her father's attention. At age 37,

Christina died in 1988, by what was determined to be a heart attack brought on by years of drug abuse.

An interesting sidenote about Jackie Kennedy that is shared by women of Ghislaine Maxwell's generation can be found in an observation made by Edith Welch – a friend of Jackie's. While working as an editor at Doubleday Jackie commissioned a book, *Indian Courtly Love*. It's about Indian courtesans who are described as a type of high-class prostitute and would could never be fully possessed by their clients. When asked by William Kuhn if Jackie had acted like a courtesan in her relationship with Jack Kennedy, Aristotle Onassis and Maurice Tempelsman, Edith replied, "You might have something there." Jacqueline Kennedy-Onassis was a well-educated woman, spoke four languages, and was always reading, but somehow she ended up marrying for money and relying on a man to take care of her. And while she wasn't Anna Nicole Smith marrying an 89-year-old wheelchair bound tycoon – she essentially did the same thing. This is something modern women may have trouble understanding.

I include this here because I view Ghislaine Maxwell's relationships with men based on the theory of being a man's courtesan. It wasn't just the women around her who were behaving in this manner – her mother, Betty, also appeared to have given herself over to her husband in the same type of submissive manner.

≈

In 1979 at the age of 18 Ghislaine Maxwell moves on from Headington Girls' School to the third of four schools she will attend in her lifetime, Marlborough College.

The school sits on 286 acres of beautifully manicured rolling grounds on the outskirt of a quaint market town in Wiltshire, England. It has red-brick classrooms, a large elegant church for Sunday services, and assigns pupils to one of their *Houses* upon entering the school. These have names like *Ivy House*, *Littlefield* and *Cotton*.

The girls wore uniforms that harkened back to the Victorian era – floor length black skirts with matching long sleeve black jackets. The evenings, however, were more relaxed in the students' dress code. There were plenty of invitations to dinner parties in elegant homes and when the school threw a party it was not uncommon for the dance floor to be full of gyrating teenagers dancing to the sounds of a live DJ.

A story I heard from the sister of twin brothers at Marlborough College when Ghislaine was a student was that she dated one of the twins. However, she veered off the subject and began to vent about the paltry salaries the housemistresses received. At the time it was £21,000 per year. "It's a disgrace," she added emphatically in disgust.

Robert Maxwell would have been horrified had he known his precious daughter whom he had managed to keep at arm's distance away from all the horrid boys who buzzed around her was partying at the expensive university with boys that clearly wanted her for one thing: sex.

But he continued to indulge her. While a student she led a life of wealth and privilege. Filipino servants were regularly dispatched to the house Ghislaine shared with some of her schoolmates to clean, do her laundry, and cook whenever she wanted to throw a party. Their services did not end there—they also set the table and served. They only left after everything was left spotless.

Marlborough College as it turns out is the same boarding school Kate Middleton, future Queen of England, attended. It's known to be a favorite of the British elite. A source snipped, "Let me explain something to you about Marlborough College, given that I went to a rival independent boarding school nearby. It makes perfect sense that both Ghislaine Maxwell and Kate Middleton were alumnae, because it caters to the aspiring upper-classes and arrivestes."

Another alum is Prince Beatrice, daughter of Prince Andrew. On June 14, 2008 the *Evening Standard* published an article entitled, *Eugenie: Dancing around without any clothes*. Apparently she had been reprimanded by her public school after she was involved in "high jinks" towards the end of her school term.

At 18, the A level student was caught running around the grounds naked. She with a dozen other students were shrieking so loudly they awakened startled staff members.

Three years previously on May 12, 2005 there were other scandals at the school while Princess Eugenie was a pupil. One headline read, *College rocked by new sex scandal*. Andrew Richards, the housemaster of CS House was arrested after police found porn on his computer.

But there have been other sex scandals at the prestigious school. In 2003 Mark Davies, the swimming pool manager was arrested after indecent pictures were found on his computer.

And in 2002 Richard Jowett, while giving an exam, unknowingly projected images of naked women onto the screen. He had busied himself with porn believing he had privacy.

Malburians, as the students are known, are like other teenagers everywhere. They experimented with drugs, smoked cigarettes, sneaked in alcohol in various ways – sometimes pouring out the contents of a shampoo bottle and replacing it with liquor before sneaking off to nightclubs. They were also extremely sexually active hopping from one partner to another.

≈

From Marlborough Robert Maxwell then sends Ghislaine to Balliol College, Oxford University. She wins a place at the school as a *Maxwell Scholar* – thanks to a scholarship scheme her father set up to fund poor students. Maxwell throughout his life managed to get everything without paying much, if anything, out of his own pocket. Even Ghislaine's Oxford education appears to have been done in a shady transaction that may very well have been written off as a tax-deductible expense.

While at college her father did not allow her to bring home boyfriends because he feared any man who was interested in her had to be a gold digger and only out for his money. Few things parted Robert Maxwell with his money. Even the gifts he gave the various women he slept with were deducted as business expenses.

≈

In December 1982 Ghislaine celebrated her 21st birthday at a large party her parents held for her at

Headington Hill Hall. Young men who hadn't been allowed to visit previously streamed into the party and were greeted by a beaming Ghislaine. Almost everyone she knew at Oxford attended. The offspring of some of the most powerful people in the U.K. danced under the over-sized chandeliers to the fast tempo music or slow danced in a tight embrace kissing with reckless abandon as if they were at one of their favorite private clubs. A live DJ played music as the Maxwell's maids and the butler moved smoothly in and out carrying trays and serving champagne with hors d'oeuvres.

At 11 p.m. that evening, to everyone's dismay, the lights first dimmed and then shut off. Her father didn't like their choice in music and decided party-time was over. Those who'd taken off their shoes scurried back into them. They formed a line as they shouted to each other giggling slipping back into and being escorted to the door. As they left they shouted back to a mournful Ghislaine, "Happy Birthday, Ghi!"

She may very well have been hurt by how her party turned out, but this did not change the deep love she felt for her father.

In a photograph taken a couple of months later during the 1982-83 Football League known as the "Milk Cup" when her father was seeking sponsors, she sits demurely alongside him as he holds up the giant silver trophy.

Tom Bower who has written two books on Robert Maxwell claims Ghislaine earned the nickname *The Shopper* because of her unrestrained use of her father's money and her insatiable appetite for new things. "He encouraged her to adopt his worst characteristics of arrogance and rudeness, tempered by charm when required. She also inherited her father's lust for wealth and power."

Bower, who has known her since she was 11 said that all her life she has "worshipped rich, domineering men."

EIGHT

Captain Bob's Ghislaine

———————

In 1982 Robert Maxwell purchased Oxford United, a football club near bankruptcy. After Ghislaine's graduation in 1984 he made the 22-year-old one of the board's directors. She had become a fixture sitting next to her father in the director's box multiple times.

In an interview, Ghislaine revealed that when she was at Balliol College she'd created a club which boasted 160 members and had arranged for them to get discounts to attend the matches.

She loved that the national press dubbed her "the most attractive director in the league." And she wasn't shy about promoting the club.

In a short interview, Ghislaine is quoted as saying, "There's more to football than watching a match. When you have a good crowd atmosphere, there is nothing better—it's electric." Then added, "If you are enthusiastic and you can get that enthusiasm across, it acts by osmosis. You can feel it. The players feel it."

She also said, "There are hundreds of families out there – a huge, untapped market for supporters. There are a lot of people for whom football is the core of their life. I'd like to make the club as successful as I can for their sake."

During this period Robert Maxwell obtained for his daughter a house at 69 Stanhope Mews East in the South Kensington area of London. It is listed as her address on the official company documents for Oxford United Football Club, registered under #00470509. In the United Kingdom football is what the Americans refer to as soccer. She resigned on December 5, 1991 – the day her father died.

The Oxford United Football Club is a publicly traded company with the President at the time being John Spencer-Churchill, 11th Duke of Marlborough – cousin of Diana Frances Spencer, Princess of Wales. Robert Maxwell followed with the title of Chairman, Director – although the title of Chairman was given to Maxwell's son, Kevin, when he was inactive on the Board as well as P. Morrissey who alternated and retired by rotation after which they would offer themselves for re-election as per the company records.

With so many of the people in Ghislaine's orbit overlapping with those in Jeffrey Epstein's life, it is of interest that the 12th Duke of Marlborough became one of Donald Trump's advisors during his Presidency.

Charles James Spencer-Churchill, the 12th Duke of Marlborough is also related to Sir Winston Churchill and Diana, Princess of Wales. Additionally he is the stepbrother of the late Christina Onassis, who was the stepdaughter of Jacqueline Kennedy Onassis, who was married to U.S. President John F. Kennedy. These names show up repeatedly in almost every conspiracy throughout history.

The Duke had a severe drug addiction and was known as the black sheep of the family. According to the *Telegraph*, in 1995 he spent a month in jail for forging prescriptions to feed his habit. He also admitted to incidents of road rage, while tailgating other drivers at high speed and once jumping out of his car to kick the door of another passenger's car. His father ultimately ended their relationship because of his son's philandering and criminal ways.

However, the Duke and Donald Trump, according to several mainstream media articles, have been "secret" friends speaking on the phone "late into the night, comparing their wild bachelor days, and visiting each other's homes."

After Oxford, Ghislaine joined her father's company Pergamon Press at Headington and, according to an interview she gave, her duties included "doing anything from typing to managing congresses".

Nine months later, her father sent Ghislaine packing to Spain to fend for herself and sell books.

Ghislaine said of this experience, "He said go and do a useful job and come back fluent. I wouldn't say I did a brilliant job, but I did sell some books and came back fluent."

NINE

Kit-Kat Club & the Royal Family

———————

While still in her early 20s Ghislaine founded a private club for women. It was called the *Kit-Kat Club* and described as an exclusive club for the more intellectual 'It Girl'.

This seems contradictory in nature as she didn't get along with other women. Not even the women who worked for her father. During phone calls with him at this time she would meow and he would meow back. Among the members is Ophelia Field, an author.

Field wrote a book about titled *Kit-Kat Club, Friends Who Imagined a Nation* published by Harper Press in 2008. It's about how Britain was '*re-branded*' in the late 17th century. The summary on her website reads:

"The Kit-Kat Club was founded in the late 1690s when Jacob Tonson, a bookseller of lowly birth, forged a partnership with the pie-maker Christopher (Kit) Cat. What began as an eccentric publishing rights deal – Tonson paying to feed hungry young writers and so receiving his first option on their works – developed into a unique gathering of intellects and interests, including famous figures such as John Vanbrugh, Willian Congreve, Joseph, Addison, Richard Steele and Robert Walpole."

On Field's website there are several pdf files available for download all pertaining to the contents of the book and the Kit-Kat Club. In one of these named *In and Out: An Analysis of Kit-Kat Club Membership* states:

"There are four main primary sources with regard to membership of the Kit-Cat Club – Abel Boyer's 1722

list, John Oldmixon's 1735 list, a Club subscription list dated 1702, and finally the portraits painted by Sir Godfrey Kneller between 1697 and 1721 (as well as the 1735 Faber engravings of these paintings). None of the sources agree. Indeed, only the membership of four men (Dr Garth, Lord Cornwallis, Spencer Compton and Abraham Stanyan) is confirmed by all four of these sources.

John Macky, a Whig journalist and spy, was the first source for the statement that the club could have no more than thirty-nine members at any one time and Malone and Spence followed suit."

I decided to go in search of Mr. Macky, the spy, and found a little information. His date of birth is unknown however he died in 1726 and was known as a government agent or spy. He was also an author having written among other books *Memoirs of Secret Services* during the reign of King William, Queen Anne, and King George. He was a Scotsman of good education but that nothing of his parentage or birth is known. There is a brief description of his own account whereby he discovered that the French government intended to send an expedition against England in 1692. However he arrived in London with the information before the army and was able to give the government ample time for preparations against it.

The purpose of the original *Kit-Kat Club* was political. By ensuring the Protestant succession, reducing French influence on national life and strengthening parliament, they aimed to "rebrand" Britain. By 1715 their objectives had largely been met and the club began to dissolve.

In Ghislaine Maxwell's now scrubbed *'LinkedIn'* profile she describes herself as a business consultant and a social media marketing expert. It's worth noting that from her earliest days she has altered her profession. At one time she even said she was an internet operator.

I found few articles about the *Kit-Kat Club*. One from 1996 and another dated 2004 which I include here.

In 1996 in the *Daily News* writes:

"Ghislaine Maxwell, daughter of late media czar Robert Maxwell, lashed out Thursday night at novelist Jeffrey Archer.

Ghislaine admitted she hadn't read "Fourth Estate," Archer's thinly veiled best seller based on the rise and fall of her father.

"Why bother? She said, "it's fiction – just like the earlier 'biographies' which purported to be nonfiction.

Ghislaine, whose father briefly owned the Daily News, added that it's no surprise that Archer's Rupert Murdoch-type character emerges a hero: "Murdoch is publishing his book."

Archer recently had the temerity to speak in London at the Kit-Kat Club, an all-female debating society founded by Ghislaine. "I had the time of my life, surrounded by women under 40," he wrote afterward. "I had orgasm after orgasm just talking to them!"

Ghislaine got in her licks against Archer at a Fashion Café party for Verve magazine, just launched by India Hicks, daughter of India's last viceroy, Lord Mountbatten. Among the guests: top Knopf editor Sonny Mehta and Sigourney Weaver, who paid homage to subcontinental style by painting her toenails a different color."

In 2004 there's another:

2004. Kit-Kat Club at The Physic Garden London – July 5: (EMBARGOED FOR PUBLICATION IN UK TABLOID NEWSPAPER UNTIL 48 HOURS AFTER CREATE DATE AND TIME). (L_R) TV presenter Andrew Neil, actress Fiona Macpherson and Lord Jeffrey Archer attend the Kit-Kat Club garden party, founded by Ghislaine Maxwell, to help women in commerce and industry at The Physic Garden, Chelsea July 5, 2004 in London."

Ghislaine's *Kit-Kat Club* does not have an official corporate document of having been officially formed. However it does have a website called kitcatclub (dot) co (dot) uk. And on its home page it refers to themselves as *'The Thinking Women's Club'*.

A portion of their 'About Us' page states, *"The Kit Cat – London's premier speaker and discussion club for women, celebrated its 30th anniversary this year. It has progressed from its early years of connecting women to ideas and inspirations from the worlds of art, science, politics, economics and philosophy that they would not necessarily otherwise encounter in their lives and careers, to its current incarnation as a focal point for women's networks, particularly those helping women starting out in their careers."*

There is, however, no mention of its founder, Ghislaine Maxwell, on the website of the *Kit-Kat Club*.

The Royal Family

In 1983-1984 Robert Maxwell began to boost his daughter's social visibility having her host corporate parties and acting as *The Mirror's* poster girl in one promotion after another. She became his unofficial goodwill ambassador. Smiling pretty for the camera. Everywhere. Even in the promotional videos he has to promote his business one catches glimpses of Ghislaine.

Photos of her during this period adorned the pages of his newspaper and probably helped to soften his public image as a ruthless womanizer hungry for power into more of a father figure and family man.

Robert Maxwell replaced his wife Betty with his youngest daughter even when attending public functions. He took her to the White House. He took her to the Kremlin. He took her to Israel. He introduced her to the men who run the world and to the shadowy people with whom he did business.

It's hard to tell whether Betty was troubled by this. Their marriage was long over—this was painfully known to all who knew them. This didn't alter her public persona. She played the role of Mrs. Robert Maxwell to the very end.

As Betty had done from the couple's early days, she dutifully added any press coverage of her husband and now her youngest to her ever-expanding collection of photo albums. Ghislaine, having grown accustomed to watching her mother clip articles and collect photos, began compiling her own.

Robert Maxwell loved being photographed with the royals. A 1983 photograph of him with Queen Elizabeth was proudly displayed at Headington Hill Hall. It is accompanied by many others. He stands next to Prince Charles, or Princess Diana, or the tragically unhappy couple together. His colossus girth and wolfish smile an odd juxtaposition to the effortless glamour of the royals.

Always scheming, with an eye on the future, Maxwell knew this would make him look even more important when Charles ascended to the throne and became King.

Prince Charles, on the other hand, was put off by the overbearing newspaper baron. On one occasion after dutifully shaking hands with the obese man he whispered to Maxwell's companion—one of his many employees, "Do tell, what is it like to work for him?"

Ghislaine Maxwell had become accustomed to accompanying her father everywhere. She called him "Daddy" and when speaking to people she would refer to him constantly as "My daddy". Throughout her life Ghislaine would speak about her father in glowing tones. Some, who sat opposite her at parties or dinner, have complained she bored them to tears as all she talked about was her father. One remarked, "There was little substance there other than a daddy's girl".

Princess Diana and the Temple of Doom

Princess Diana wore a pale blue Catherine Walker gown on June 11, 1984 when she and Prince Charles attended the premiere of *Indiana Jones and the Temple of Doom* at the Empire Cinema in Leicester Square, London. She is pregnant with her second child expected to arrive in September.

In a photograph Ghislaine is seen standing on the receiving line with her brothers Kevin and Ian as well as the film's producer, Steven Spielberg. She is shaking Princess Diana's hand as the two smile cordially at one another.

The film is about child abduction and human sacrifice. Indiana Jones, after surviving a murder attempt by a crime boss in Shanghai, flees with his sidekick *Short Round* and the nightclub singer *Willie Scott*. The three arrive in the fake village of Mayapore in northern India. The villagers plead for their aid in retrieving a sacred stone that was stolen from their shrine along with their missing children by evil forces in nearby Pankot Palace. Ultimately the trio reach an underground temple where the *Thugge* cult worships the Hindu goddess Kali by sacrificing the missing children.

～

Princess Diana was tragically killed in a car accident in the early morning hours of August 31, 1997. Her funeral was held on September 6 at Westminster Abbey. While rewatching the funeral I noticed a woman who looked like Ghislaine Maxwell in the audience. After confirming it was indeed Maxwell I searched for others. While there is no official guest list for who was there I discovered Steven Spielberg and Hillary Clinton were in attendance.

In 1997 Bill Clinton was President of the United States and Hillary, First Lady. Working in Clinton's White House was a family friend of Ghislaine Maxwell, namely, Leah Pisar.

Pisar was selected by Bill Clinton to become the Director of Communications at the National Security Council (NSC). She is the daughter of Samuel Pisar who was Robert Maxwell's longtime advisor and attorney. Robert Maxwell and Samuel Pisar formed a very tight friendship that lasted well beyond Maxwell's death. Leah Pisar's half-brother, Antony Blinken, also had a position at Clinton's National Security Council (NSC) at the same time.

During President Barack Obama's administration, Blinken became Deputy Assistant to the President and National Security Advisor to Vice President Joe Biden.

Joe Biden won the presidential election against incumbent President Donald Trump on November 3, 2020. He selected Antony Blinken as the new Secretary of State.

Ghislaine Maxwell has friends in high places in many countries. However, when one studies who sits in what position and becomes familiar with the names in Jeffrey Epstein's black book, it appears to echo the purpose of the original Kit-Kat Club. The re-branding of a country—this time the United States of America.

TEN

Good Time Ghislaine

Annabel's is a private members only club in Mayfair, located West of London. It was founded in 1963 by Mark Birley then married to Lady Annabel Vane-Tempest-Stewart after whom he named it. Annabel would later marry Sir Jimmy Goldsmith, rumored to be a spy, and who, in the early 1970s became a friend of Jeffrey Epstein's.

It was the first of its kind—a club for the very affluent, the very powerful or the very famous. Their clientele included the royal family. Charles, Prince of Wales who everyone believed would be King in short order and his younger brother, Prince Andrew. It was the only club that Queen Elizabeth ever attended. In later years it became the go-to club for younger royals like Princes William and Harry.

The entrance was lined even from the earliest days with the rich, the powerful and the beautiful where streams of the upper-class descended into the basement to party. Journalists were never admitted and the entertainment included The Rolling Stones, Diana Ross and in earlier days Ella Fitzgerald. Joan Collins was in the club dancing one evening and a photographer from *The Sun* had managed to get himself into the club. He snapped a photo of her and was immediately plucked off the dance floor by two burly men who left him lying on the pavement outside sans the film in his camera.

After tumbling down the stairs into the poshest basement on the planet one is welcome into a den of hedonistic indulgence. The rooms were covered in wild wallpaper along with paintings by Picasso and racy nude drawings. The bathroom sinks were in the shape of golden swans and the walls a sensual floral pink. A life size gorilla sitting on a chair stood guard at the end of the hallway. It was over the top eccentric, but most of all it was posh.

In the 1980s Ghislaine Maxwell was one of the *somebodies* along with her friends from Oxford. As with the debutantes of days long gone Ghislaine would murmur, "Take me to Bel's" to the man of the moment. And, one of her men in the 1980s was David Faber – a future MP.

Annabel's was the sort of place where anything went and where smooching in one of dozens of its nooks and crannies was as much a part of the experience as kicking off one's shoes or one's clothes and losing oneself to the pulsating euphoria of the music on the infamous wooden dancefloor.

David Faber is a descendent of several British politicians. He also happens to be the great-grandson of the founder of MacMillan Publishing.

More tidbits about David include that his that uncle, Maurice Macmillan, worked with Sir Edward Heath during the time he was Prime Minister. Heath is alleged to have sexually abused children commencing in 1961. He served for 51 years as a member of Parliament and died in 2005.

It should be noted that MacMillan was taken over by Robert Maxwell in November of 1988 for $2.6

billion. Although Maxwell claimed he had no plans to dispose of the company's assets, one month later he sold a piece of it, Intertec, to an investment group led by Rothschild, Inc – the same company that served as his adviser in the purchase. Robert S. Pirie the Co-Chairman and CEO of Rothschild North America was his advisor in the transaction. In 1993 Pirie went on to became the Senior Managing Director of Bear Stearns & Co.

I thought it interesting that all the people in Maxwell's world circled around to those in Epstein's world and so I tracked down an old *New York Times* article. It states:

"Bear Stearns hired Mr. Pirie as a senior managing director. The firm, known primarily for trading, is trying to increase its banking business."

A 1984 photo of David Faber dragging a disheveled and unbalanced 22-year-old Ghislaine while holding up her arm attempting to keep her steady on her feet at Annabel's exists. It was taken by Dafydd Jones who worked at Tatler magazine from 1981 through 1989.

Jones, armed with a discreet camera and a dinner jacket to blend into the crowd, took some of the best photographs of Britain's high society at the time. He said, "A lot of the dramas and important moments in people's lives happen during parties." His collection includes young and sloppy drunken parties with fully clothed debutantes pushed into lily ponds and swimming pools. "They were living in a bubble," he explained. "it was cool to be wearing black tie and dressing up in reaction against relaxed style which had gone before in the 70s."

While Annabel's always maintained a "no photo" policy banishing any member who breached protocol, nowadays with the advent of social media, their house rule has morphed into: *"Photography within the club and posting to social media should be discreet and not involve or feature other members and their guests."*

Ghislaine and David began their romance while both at Balliol College, Oxford University. I was able to find a second photograph also taken by Dafydd Jones of Faber with Maxwell at the Chelsea Arts Ball during the club's extravagant New Year's Eve party on December 31, 1985. And there were probably many more before all things Maxwell began to get scrubbed off the internet after Jeffrey Epstein's second arrest on July 6, 2019.

Ghislaine's father, Bob, who had already cozied up to the Royal family and was fond of having his photo taken with Prince Charles, Princess Diana and the Queen would have been delighted to know Ghislaine was dancing up a storm and rubbing elbows with the royals.

Prince Andrew was also a frequent guest at Annabel's which is an 8-minute drive to another one of his favorite clubs: Tramp.

The Chelsea Arts Club is another private members club established in 1891. To be considered as a member one needs to be sponsored by two current members. It was known for its hedonism where literally anything was allowed. Nudity, sex, homosexuality at a time when it wasn't the norm – everything happened behind the ever-changing murals hand-painted by their resident artists.

Ghislaine wasn't the only woman David romanced. While at Oxford he also dated Sally Gilbert, a leggy blonde, who is said by a contemporary of his to have "pursued him with great determination – he didn't have a chance." She became a television weather girl and they married in 1988.

By 1992 Sally had fallen out of love with David finding him to be lacking in warmth and found herself being comforted by the world's most celebrated cad, James Hewitt. Faber when filing for divorce cited James Hewitt as co-respondent.

Major Hewitt, it should be noted, was Princess Diana's riding teacher and in the Household Cavalry when tasked to give her riding lessons. Hewitt, while romancing Farber's soon to be ex-wife, revealed himself as having a five-year affair with Princess Diana that began in 1986. To avoid getting caught Diana used the codename 'Julia' when sending mail to Hewitt.

Hewitt told the world, via a book co-authored with British journalist Anna Pasternak, that he was Princess Diana's lover in 1994 when she was still married to Prince Charles, the future King of England. Diana was bitterly hurt and devasted when she learned he had shopped around the story of their affair. Although there are claims she continued to see him afterwards up to several months before her untimely death in Paris on August 31, 1997.

Ghislaine Maxwell was not considered a good student during her time at Oxford, not by her professors and not even by herself. She did however earn the nickname "Good Time Ghislaine". This suited her just fine.

In 2010 David Faber became the tenth Headmaster of Summer Field School in Oxford. It is a boarding school for boys aged 4-13. The bio on the school's page reads, "He is an old boy of the School, a former parent and had previously served as a Governor for nine years. He teaches History, with a particular expertise in the Second World War and the history of appeasement.

After attending Summer Fields, along with many other members of his family, David Faber was educated at Eton and Balliol College, Oxford, where he read Modern Languages, played 2nd XI cricket and won a half-blue for rackets. After university he worked for the Conservative party in a number of roles, before contesting the Stockton North constituency unsuccessfully at the 1987 General Election. He was elected to Parliament in 1992 for the Westbury seat in West Wiltshire, which he held for nine years."

His name is in Jeffrey Epstein's black book.

From the awkward looking teenager Ghislaine had grown into an adult. She seemed taller than her height, perhaps because of her heels, or how she carried herself. The youngest daughter of Robert Maxwell is described by those who knew her as thin with broad shoulders and thick black layered hair. Her complexion is pale and her fingernails are regularly manicured with crimson red nail polish. One person added, "she had an intense sexuality, an almost androgynous allure."

Robert Maxwell was fond of saying, "I have a "beautiful daughter who is just like me."

ELEVEN

Blackmail & Spankings

On October 26, 1986 23-year-old Ghislaine Maxwell's face appeared on the front cover of one of her father's U.K. gossip publications *The People*. The article claimed someone had tried to blackmail Robert

Maxwell for his on-going coverage of MP Harry Proctor's child sex spanking scandal.

In large bold letters the size usually reserved for the death of a King of Queen the headline read, *BLACKMAIL, Maxwell threatened over spanking M.P.*

In 1986 at the age of 24 (oddly, the article claims she was 23) Ghislaine found herself in the midst of a blackmail attempt involving a child abuse ring of high-profile men such as MP Harvey Proctor.

The article reads:

"Astonishing threats have been made to The People and to publisher Robert Maxwell following our exposure of spanking MP Harvey "Whacko" Proctor.

A sinister phone caller said that if we continued with our "campaign" against the kinky MP he would reveal compromising details of an alleged relationship between Mr. Maxwell's daughter Ghislaine and the son of a duke. The anonymous male caller, who tried to get through to Mr. Maxwell, told his receptionist:

'I will produce a story about Ghislaine and Lord Granby at Belvoir castle with incriminating pictures of them in compromising positions.'

He threatened 'other dire consequences.'

Last night Mr. Maxwell said: 'He was told in no uncertain terms to get lost. The People and its publisher will not be frightened.'

The 26-year-old Marquis of Granby, heir to the Duke of Rutland, said last night: 'I find all this slightly alarming. Ghislaine Maxwell is a very dear friend to me and that's as far as it goes.'

Of the caller's claim that he had incriminating pictures showing the peer with 23-year-old Miss Maxwell, the Marquis said: 'That is lot of nonsense—a load of rubbish. Our friendship is purely innocent.

'Ghislaine comes to our family home in London for drinks sometimes, and we have had dinner together. So what!' There is NO suggestion that the blackmail call was made or instigated by Mr Proctor.

The Tory MP for Billericay said at his home in Fulham last night: "I know nothing about it at all. I would describe this kind of threat as absolutely disgraceful.

I have no idea who would do anything like that. It has nothing to do with me. I have nothing more to say. "The People's investigation into Proctor's sex life began in June, when homosexual David Jackson came to us with allegations about his affair with Tory MP.

Jackson also produced a number of obscene photographs of naked boys which he claimed had been taken by Proctor after he had beaten them with a cane, a slipper and his hand.

Proctor, confronted by the People, confirmed the photographs had been taken in his Fulham flat and that Jackson had stayed at his flat.

But he strongly denied allegations of beating boys in sex fantasy games in which he played the role of headmaster. At a recent meeting of the Billericay Conservative Association senior executive council members resigned in protest after Proctor was given a vote of support.

On the basis of our evidence, Scotland Yard's Serious Crimes Squad is now conducting its own investigation.

On October 12, The People ran a leader saying Proctor was not fit to remain an MP.

It concluded: 'In the words of Oliver Cromwell 'IN THE NAME OF GOD, GO!'.'

MP Harvey Proctor, in one newspaper account after another, was alleged to be having sex with minor boys. Boys that were part of a trafficking ring. Boys referred to as "prostitutes" or "rentboys". One such minor said that Proctor used the popular game *Trivial Pursuits* to act out his sexual fantasies.

If the boy answered incorrectly he would be punished and beaten with a cane. Proctor is also alleged by this victim and others that he loved taking Polaroid photographs of them in the nude. One of the men who supplied young boys to Proctor said, "I could not count the number of boys I supplied to Harvey over a three-year period. It cost him a small fortune".

One boy would be asked to bring another boy into the trafficking ring. Among these Jason Burton, then 17, who "met a skinhead at Earles Court underground station who then introduced him to Proctor at his home in July 1986. According to Burton there was another boy there. He alleges that Proctor took him into his bedroom and asked him if he had ever been caned at school.

He replied he had.

Proctor instructed him to leave the room and to knock on the door.

Upon re-entering the room he was told by Proctor to get undressed and put on a pair of white shorts. He was then instructed him to call Proctor "Sir" while receiving his punishment and having sex.

During his second encounter with Proctor he was "punished for fighting in class".

Others told the same tale. "I'm headmaster, call me Sir," Proctor instructed before engaging in his usual sexual fantasies with boys not yet of age.

In 1987 Harvey Proctor was forced to resign as MP for Billericay after being fined £1,450 for gross acts of indecency. According to newspaper reports the cause was for "homosexual spanking sessions with young male prostitutes".

One victim lived in a state-run care facility for boys. He disclosed that a man would come around and pick him and some other boys up. The group of boys would be taken to apartments where Proctor would be waiting with other men. During these trysts the boys were often tied up, photographed and then raped.

Other young men stepped forward with claims against the beleaguered Proctor, as well as Jimmy Savile. Savile was revealed after his death to be among the world's most heinous pedophiles.

Proctor opened up a shirt shop in Brewers Lane, Off Richmond Green in 1988. To do so he obtained a £2,000 grant from the Government's Enterprise Allowance Scheme and procured help from other men who had also suffered reversals in their political careers. As per an article in the Times dated March 1993:

"These included Neil Hamilton, forced to resign as Northern Ireland minister last week after allegations that he was rewarded by Mohamed Al Fayed, owner of Harrods, for helping in his battle with Tiny Rowland; Tim Yeo, the former Environment minister who was

forced to resign after news broke of his adultery with Julia Stent, a Hackney Labour councillor, who bore his child; Michael Brown, who resigned as a Tory whip last May after a tabloid newspaper reported his homosexual affairs with a youth and a Ministry of Defense civil servant; and David Ashby, who suffered unwelcome publicity after admitting sleeping with a man but denying having sexual relations with him."

～

Favors, it appears, were called in to help former MP Harvey Proctor. His shirt shop however did not do well.

In 2003 Proctor became the private secretary to David Manners, 11th Duke of Rutland at his home, Belvoir Castle, at Leicestershire.

Manners has had a very colorful sex life. He married late in life at the age of 33 in 1992 when he wed Emma Watkins. They promptly had five children. In 2012 she filed for divorce after catching him having an affair with Andrea Webb, who lived on the couple's 15,000 square foot acre estate.

In 2017 the Duke of Rutland called the police to escort his lover off the premises after he "disinvited" Webb from a party. She was escorted off Belvoir Castle.

The Duke appears by press reports to be a man with an insatiable sexual appetite. Ghislaine is rumored to be equally passionate. In an August 9, 2020 article in *The Sun* with the title *Love to brag Ghislaine Maxwell boasted about performing sex act on George Clooney,'* as told to them by one of her alleged victims reads:

"Citing court documents of a deposition given by Virginia Giuffre, 'One time she came back giddy as a schoolgirl with an explosion of news, with all the build-up and excitement in her voice you'd think she was the next crown princess,' Giuffre wrote of Maxwell in her book, which was unsealed by a New York judge last week.

'But she had given George Clooney a b–w j-b in the bathroom at some random event. ... She never let that one down.'"

At the time of the publication of the *BLACKMAIL* story in 1986 with Ghislaine Maxwell on the cover, over 90% of the readers thought all of it was a lie created by Robert Maxwell in order to sell more papers. This is a typical response because no one wants to believe these things actually happen.

David Manners, the above-named son of the Duke, was among the people whose name and phone numbers were found in Jeffrey Epstein's black book.

≈

Oddly, in 1986 Ghislaine was summoned by her father to a Dutch shipyard to take a bottle of the finest champagne and smash it across the hull of his new yacht *The Lady Ghislaine.* Ghislaine was giddy with excitement that of all the siblings it was she he had chosen to name his new toy after.

Maxwell purchased it from Adnan Khashoggi's nephew, Emad. Emad is also the cousin of journalist Jamal Khashoggi who was murdered and cut into pieces by the Saudis in October 2018. The vessel was equipped with the latest satellite system which allowed Maxwell to conduct business on international waters and evade the laws of any country.

TWELVE

Count Gianfranco Cicogna

———————

The great love of Ghislaine Maxwell's life was Count Gianfranco Cicogna. Born on September 29, 1962 Cicogna was a handsome and dashing member of the CIGA (Compagnia Italiana Grandi Alberghi) hotel clan. Their love affair lasted four years – from 1986 to 1990. At which point the Count ditched Ghislaine for TV weather girl Tania Bryer.

All photos of Ghislaine and Cicogna have been scrubbed off the internet. I managed to salvage two of them. At one time there was a Wikipedia page for Count Gianfranco Cicogna – however, that too, has disappeared.

Cicogna is credited for having molded Ghislaine Maxwell into the sleek socialite the world would soon see. He told her where to get her hair cut and what to wear. For a young woman with access to as much money as she could spend, she didn't have an innate sense of style. Ghislaine was, by all accounts, incredibly in love with him. She was sure they would marry and she would become his Contessa.

The enterprising Cicogna was often referred to in the press as Italy's Rockefeller. He inherited his title at the age of 10 when his father died. His grandfather, Count Giuseppe Volpi di Misurata, was the Italian Minister of finance between 1910 and 1950, the last Doge of Venice and governor of North Africa.

Volpi di Misurata was one of the wealthiest men in Italy, if not the world. He owned railroads, electrical companies, hotels and nearly everything in Venice. He was also a Freemason and a fascist. By 1907 he was one of the largest shareholders of CIGA which already owned the Hotel Excelsior in Venice.

One year later Volpi's two-year-old CIGA was able to take over the hotel from Societa Bagni Lida. He transformed it into the world's most prestigious tourist get-away. In 1912 Financier Pierpont Morgan said, "in America, those who have visited Europe talk more of the Excelsior Palace than they do of the Doge's Palace".

The hotel's illustrious guests included Albert II of Belgium the Duke of Windsor (Prince Andrew's uncle), Winston Churchill, Barbara Hutton and countless movie stars. Hedy Lamarr and her husband Fritz Mandi spent the first night of their honeymoon there. In 1925 Volpi was granted the title of Count of Misurata by Victor Emmanuel III, then King of Italy.

Count Gianfranco Cicogna loved flying. It is perhaps because of him that Ghislaine learned to fly. He studied international economics and could speak five languages. He became enchanted by Africa after spending a scuba diving holiday in Kenya. It led to his starting an export firm in Kenya supplying European customers with fruits and vegetables. He then expanded to South America. His professional career was an odd mix: international banking, marketing and farming.

A drug scandal and a murder

The scandalous past of his father, Giuseppe Ascanio Cicogna Mozzoni, aside from having died—either from suicide or murder—when Gianfranco was a young boy of 10 is less known. Referred to among his peers as Bino Cignona in 1962 he married Gioconda Gallardo Moreno with whom he had two children and from whom he separated quickly. Bino was in the film industry, produced several movies and was a screenwriter. The films had notable movie stars including Eli Wallach who played the leading role in 'Ace High' in 1968. However, because of his spending habits by 1971 Cignona's film company Finanziaria San Marco was inundated with debts.

Bino Cicogna and actress Britt Ekland were photographed at the Golden Awards in Film Gala on October 11, 1969 in Brigadoon in Rome, Italy.

Bino Cignona's best friend was Pierre Luigi Torre – another playboy from an aristocratic family who, like Cignona, was involved with the film industry – in his case, however, he produced soft-porn Italian movies. The friends spent their time in expensive casinos and nightclubs bedding one beautiful girl after another.

The duo always wanted to run their own nightclub – an exclusive gambling casino for their wealthy friends.

To this end they found an old war ship and planned to refurbish it. While this didn't work out their stunt garnered a lot of press coverage giving the playboys instant recognition everywhere.

Bino Cicogna, Pierre Luigi Torre and another hedonist, Paolo Vasallo, ended up co-owning *the* club in Rome named 'Number One' located on the Via Veneto. Federico Fellini's classic 1960 film La Dolce Vita was filmed in the Via Veneto area. Today it is the most famous, elegant and most expensive street in Rome, Italy.

The atmosphere of Club One was a precursor to Studio 54. Their clientele were among the most prestigious families, well-known actors and actresses, as well as the politicians of their day. No expense was spared in making their evenings of debauchery complete. Cocaine was part of the cocktail menu. It was delivered with drinks to the tables with the use of a special code.

In 1971 the Number One club was raided by the police and busted for cocaine. Many notable people were arrested including the owners. Bino fled to Rio de Janeiro, Brazil and Pierre Luigi got on his yacht and sailed first to Monaco and then to London.

By December Bino Cicogna, Gianfranco's father, was found dead. The cause of death was labeled suicide.

Bino was found with his head, covered with a bag, in the oven. The authorities claimed he was distraught over having become addicted to cocaine and the pending criminal charges against him. Pierre Luigi didn't believe Bino would have committed suicide. He suspected murder.

The "Number One Scandal" was a big deal. It included a lot of famous people and was in all the newspapers at the time. Tales of cocaine fueled orgies, abnormal sex, suicides and murders kept the Italian public fascinated for years.

However, almost everything about this scandal, which was alleged to have the involvement of organized crime, has been scrubbed off the internet.

The break-up

The affair between Ghislaine Maxwell and Count Gianfranco Cicogna is remembered as a "passionate" one. It lasted four years ending in 1990 – just one year before the mysterious death of her father Robert Maxwell. When Cicogna left her for another woman, Ghislaine responded in typical scorned woman fashion. Her photo appeared in newspapers with a revolving door of womanizing men. Perhaps she was hoping to ignite envy in her former lover. Among these men were Hollywood actor George Hamilton whom she met while on a first- class plane ride from New York to London. By the time the flight was over he agreed to take her to the Derby in his helicopter. The two were photographed at the event in June 1991. Another was John F. Kennedy, Jr. who she had known through her father for years.

It is worth noting there is no mention of Jeffrey Epstein after the break-up which left her heartbroken.

Count Gianfranco Cicogna's ghastly death

On a sunny Saturday morning on June 30, 2012 while flying his plane at the Klersdorp Air Show in Africa, Gianfranco Cicogna-Mozzoni died in a fiery plane crash as thousands of people watched in horror. He was 49 and left behind a wife and two children.

His was one of the many names found in Jeffrey Epstein's black book.

Ari-Ben Menashe

Ari-Ben Menashe is a one-time Mossad agent, a former arms dealer and shadowy business consultant. He has shown up on several podcasts where he claims Ghislaine Maxwell met Jeffrey Epstein in the mid-1980s and that they had "fallen in love". He further claims her father Robert Maxwell was happy to have a nice Jewish boy with money as a marriage prospect for her. And, according to Menashe, Mossad took Epstein into the fold and helped the love birds with what Menashe labeled their small enterprise. Namely, their human trafficking and blackmail business. The problem with this story is that Martin Dillon, who co-authored *Robert Maxwell, Israel's Superspy,* diligently researched Robert Maxwell and everyone who knew him for their book – including current and former members of the Mossad. Dillon claims there was no trace of Epstein.

This author echo's that finding. It is my belief they met in a way I describe in an upcoming chapter. To make it sound otherwise would be to dispel the fact that Leslie Wexner funded Jeffrey Epstein. Further it would completely erase the four years Ghislaine Maxwell spent with Count Gianfranco Cicogna. And, most of all it would create an illusion that the trafficking ring was "small". It wasn't. It isn't. It is much larger than mainstream media reports have suggested.

Victor Ostrovksy

Another "former" Mossad agent, Victor Ostrovsky has also made an appearance in the Jeffrey Epstein and Ghislaine Maxwell case. Ostrovsky was a Mossad "katsa" – a field intelligence officer who collects information and runs agents.

In 2016 Conchita Sarnoff, a former friend of both Jeffrey Epstein and Ghislaine Maxwell published a book *TrafficKing* about the Epstein case. She claims no one wanted to publish the book. With the exception of one man: Victor Ostrovsky.

THIRTEEN

Ghislaine's work assignments

1989

Alastair Campbell, who worked for Robert Maxwell as the political editor of the *Daily Mirror,* wrote about a strange assignment Maxwell sent him and Ghislaine on in 1989.

"Ghislaine had also been central to possibly the most bizarre assignment of my journalistic career – no, definitely the most bizarre assignment of my journalistic career – when Maxwell, for reasons I never fully fathomed, sent Ghislaine and I to Paris to hand over the remains of an Argentine political and military leader, Juan Manuel de Rosas, who had died in Hampshire in 1877. Bear with me. Heaven knows how The Sunday Mirror readers felt on the full-page account of this bizarre diplomatic mission intruding on their reading of sport and showbiz."

Rosas was known as *The Caligula of the River Plate* having built a ruthless secret police force, assassinating his enemies and making it a requirement for citizens to wear his colors. When his wife, Encarnacion, died in 1838 he began an affair with his 15-year-old maid, Maria Eugenia Castro, with whom he had five children.

When he was overthrown in February 1852 he fled to Buenos Aires. Once there he disguised himself and boarded a ship that sailed to Britain where he would live in exile until his death in 1877 at the age of 84. The British gave him asylum, paid for his travel and gave him a hero's welcome replete with a 21-gun salute. According to British Foreign Secretary James Harris, 3rd Earl of Malmesbury, "General Rosas was no common refugee, but one who has shown great distinction and kindness to the British merchants who had traded with his county". Rosas' family had spent 55 years trying to get Rosas' remains returned to Argentina.

It is worth noting that Ghislaine Maxwell's eldest surviving brother, Philip, described as a brilliant scientist moved to Argentina as a young man to get away from his domineering father that he loathed. Philip has authored many scientific research papers in the field of economics while living in Argentina. In an article by the *Independent* dated November 6, 2011 Philip was said to have moved back to London and gotten married for the second time.

In the book *Robert Maxwell, Israel's Superspy,* co-authored by Gordon Thomas and Martin Dillon, it states that Maxwell sold compromised versions of *Inslaw's PROMIS* software to Chile and Argentina. The software had a backdoor—a trojan horse—allowing Israel to spy in real time and see what their friends and foes were up to. It also helped them gauge the extent of how far the Latin American regimes would go in suppressing human rights and religious freedoms. PROMIS was the most reliable source of information helping Mossad monitor the cycle of war and ceasefire which helped determine the rhythm of Israeli policy.

1990

Robert Maxwell sends 29-year-old Ghislaine to a gala dinner honoring Nazi hunter Simon Wiesenthal at the Los Angeles center that bears his name and which was founded in 1977. Maxwell is a regular co-chair at this annual event which resembles a smaller version of the Academy Awards. Hollywood producers, such as Harvey Weinstein, and actors who have made films reminding the world of the atrocities Jewish people have been subjected to historically and at the Nazi concentration camps are among those honored regularly.

Robert Maxwell's schedule conflicted with the tribute as he had to go to Moscow to meet with Mikhail Gorbachev. As usual his activities were looked upon by intelligence agencies in the United States and in the United Kingdom as suspicious. Furthermore his travels to Russia were frequent. His publishing empire printed scientific research papers from leading universities in the United States in Russia behind the Iron Curtain. As early as 1962 intelligence agencies knew Maxwell was allowed to enter the Soviet Union six times a year while other people struggled to get any access.

FBI documents show continuous concern about Maxwell's activities in Russia. One reads, *"Maxwell's channel is a renegade Britisher who has lived for many years in Moscow. With the knowledge and consent of the*

USSR Academy, he, Maxwell, is appointing this man as a representative of Pergamon Press (Maxwell's publishing enterprise). Since there seems to be no interest in censorship he will use this man as a drop for communications with scientists. He has some code arranged to advise them about forthcoming invitations. He fears, however that his British official contacts will not approve the appointment of this man as his business agent. Maxwell's primary interest seems to be to get USSR cooperation for his publishing ventures."

Ghislaine and her father flew on the Concorde from London to Los Angeles where he continued on to Russia and she to her hotel. By this time Ghislaine had been working at her father's side and following his instructions for close to one decade.

The Simon Wiesenthal Tolerance Center in Los Angeles was built with a $500,000 donation from Samuel Belzberg and a matching half million from Joseph Tannenbaum. Belzberg and Tannenbaum were both Canadian entrepreneurs. Belzberg's daughter, Lisa, married Matthew Bronfman, son of Edgar Bronfman, Sr. Bronfman, like Maxwell, had business dealings with Russia. In April 1989 Robert Maxwell and Charles Bronfman joined forces to bid for a controlling interest in *The Jerusalem Post* – Israel's only English-language paper. Once again, Jeffrey Epstein and Ghislaine Maxwell's worlds intertwine. When Epstein worked at

Bear Stearns from 1975 through 1981 one of his clients was Bronfman, Sr.

It seems that sending one of his daughters in his place was commonplace as an article in the *Los Angeles Times* dated November 21, 1989 references Christine, Ghislaine's sister, as appearing on her father's behalf due to his being in ill health. The article notes that Christine delivered a "passionate speech—written by her father—which was the evening's best received".

Recipients of awards in 1989 were notable Hollywood actors and producers. Among these Mary Steenburgen (*The Attic: The Hiding of Anne Frank*); Martin Starger (*Escape From Sobibor* and *Sophie's Choice*); Arthur Cohn (*The Garden of the Finzi Continis*); Joseph Bottoms, Tovah Feldshuh, and James Woods (*Holocaust*); Stanley Kramer (*Judgment at Nuremberg*); Dan Curtis and Jane Seymour (*War and Remembrance*), and Robert Cooper, Craig T. Nelson and Ben Kingsley (*Murderers Among Us: The Simon Wiesenthal Story*).

Yitzhak Shamir, the Prime Minister of Israel saluted the movie industry for keeping the memory of the Holocaust alive. In a prepared speech he said, "As you know, our state does not happen to be located in the most friendly neighborhood. When Moses led us there he probably did not foresee the fanaticism, hatred and war that are endemic to the region. Perhaps I should have a word with Charlton Heston about that."

Ghislaine's speech was as well received as the one given by her sister, Christine, a year earlier. This was noted on the center's website where they wrote about Maxwell's youngest daughter having spoken on behalf of her father. On their website it listed the date as 1989 instead of 1990. However, the page has been removed since I first discovered it close to two years ago.

Ghislaine called her father the following morning as instructed presenting him with a review of what happened the previous evening. Instead of praise, he scolded her. In a written apology she explained, "I am very sorry that my description of the dinner this morning was inadequate and made you angry. I should have expressed at the start of our conversation that I was merely presenting you with a preliminary report of the evening and that a full written report was to follow."

She then wrote long descriptions of every guest, praised her father and signed off: "I will call you again tomorrow to receive your precise instructions for the Kennedy wedding".

Yitzhak Shamir

Yitzhak Shamir proudly proclaimed throughout his life that he had been a leader of the Zionist militant group Lehi. Files released by MI5 in December of 2017 provide new insight into a bombing campaign which terrorized London in the years following World War II. The terrorist group Lehi targeted government offices and sent letter bombs to ministers—including future Prime Minister Anthony Eden, post-war Labor Prime Minister Clement Attlee, Foreign Secretary Ernest Bevin, Chancellor Stafford Cripps and wartime Prime Minister Winston Churchill. The Lehi group were also known by British authorities as the Stern Gang. They were considered to be the most right-wing of the armed Zionists groups. At one point they even approached Hitler's Nazi Germany to work out an agreement vowing to fight for Hitler against the British in Palestine.

It was the Lehi and Irgun, another Zionist paramilitary organization, who led what is remembered as the most notorious massacre in the Palestine village of Deir Yasin, where over 100 Palestinian civilians were murdered. Many more massacres took place in later years as well.

Churchill himself – in one of his most notorious racist rants in the 1930s — said of the Palestinian people, "I do not agree that the dog in a manger has the final right to the manger even though he may have lain there for a very long time... I do not admit, for instance, that a great wrong has been done to the Red Indians of America or the black people of Australia. I do not admit that a wrong has been done to these people by the fact that a stronger race, a higher-grade race, a more worldly-wise race to put it that way, has come in and taken their place."

In the files is a press clipping of an interview with 22-year-old Betty Knouth, one of the Lehi bombers. She was sentenced to only one year in prison despite having been caught red-handed with letter bombs addressed to high-ranking British officials.

During an interview in 1948 at a conference in Tel Aviv Knouth expressed regret only because her plot was thwarted by the Belgian police. She said, "I'm sorry none of them was delivered. My terrorist days are over and done with now."

On May 29, 1948 the government of the newly formed state of Israel inducted its activist members into the Israeli Defense Forces, and disbanded Lehi. Although it is acknowledged that some of its members continued to carry out terrorist acts including the assassination of Folke Bernadotte, Count of Wisborg. Just before Israel's first elections in January 1949 amnesty was granted to Lehi members by the government. In 1980 Israel created the *Lehi Ribbon* as an "award to activity in the struggle for the establishment of Israel". Three years later Yitzhak Shamir became the Prime Minister.

Simon Wiesenthal

Simon Wiesenthal would receive many honors before his death at the age of 96 on September 20, 2005. Among the many awards are two movies based on his life.

The 1978 film *The Boys from Brazil* starring Laurence Olivier is based on him. In the movie, the aging Nazi hunter, Ezra Lieberman, learns about a secret organization of war criminals. When he begins to investigate the suspicious death of aging civil servants he meets several of their widows and discovers an uncanny resemblance in their sons. All of whom have black hair and blue eyes. As the plot unfolds it is revealed these are clones of Adolf Hitler – their mothers implanted with zygotes carrying a sample of his DNA in the 1960s.

The second in 1989 – an HBO movie *Murderers Among Us: The Simon Wiesenthal Story* based on his memoir starring Ben Kingsley.

In 1980 a teary-eyed President Jimmy Carter presented Wiesenthal with a special gold medal awarded by the United States Congress. And in 1988 President

Ronald Reagan praised him as being one of the true heroes of the century.

The Kennedy Connection

Robert Maxwell had a decades long relationship with the Kennedy family. Joseph Patrick Kennedy Sr. the patriarch of the Irish-American Kennedy family born on September 6, 1888 became the United States Ambassador to the United Kingdom in 1938 through 1940. By 1935 he was worth $180 million dollars which would be the equivalent today of $3.4 billion. Kennedy had close ties with Senator Joseph McCarthy and often invited him to the family's compound at Hyannis Port. At one point McCarthy dated his daughter, Patricia.

McCarthy and his chief aide, attorney Roy Cohn, became famous during the anti-Communist Cold War hysteria that became known as "McCarthyism" – a term coined in 1950. He and Cohn alleged there were hidden Soviet spies and sympathizers that had infiltrated the United States government, the film industry, the universities and elsewhere.

His son John F. Kennedy became President of the United States in 1960. Kennedy had the backing of the Zionists at the request of Kennedy Sr. Meshulam Riklis CEO of *Rapid American Corporation* attended a meeting at The Pierre Hotel at the request of his friend

Kennedy with several other men. They handed the young presidential hopeful $200,000 in hundred-dollar bills with instructions that once elected he had to help with Israel. This story is known to the author who was in a close relationship with Riklis's eldest son.

Robert Maxwell's Polish born attorney, Samuel Pisar, became an advisor to President John F. Kennedy. It is worth noting that Pisar's daughter Leah worked for President Bill Clinton at the State Department and as communications director at the National Security Council. His stepson, Antony Blinken, was recently selected by President Joe Biden as the Secretary of State.

Ghislaine was instructed by Robert Maxwell to attend the Kennedy weddings. She was invited to the June 10, 1990 wedding of Kerry Kennedy—daughter of assassinated Senator Robert Kennedy—and Andrew Cuomo in Washington D.C. She was photographed sitting on the lawn flirting with a grinning Joe Kennedy, Jr.

OK Magazine claims she had a one-time romp with John F. Kennedy, Jr. The source said, "It happened in the early 1990s soon after Ghislaine had started to establish herself on the New York social scene. He went to her house after a political event and she would routinely drop into the conversation. Who wouldn't right?" To this author, this further establishes the fact that Ghislaine Maxwell was not Jeffrey Epstein's girlfriend. Not in the mid-1980s, not when she arrived in New York and, frankly, not ever.

However, she may have had flings with more than one Kennedy. On December 4, 1990 *Women's Wear Daily* wrote an article titled *London Watch* covering several events for U.K. fashion designer Bruce Oldfield. Apparently Ghislaine Maxwell arrived at Zuma Restaurant after Oldfield's dinner party on the arm of Joe Kennedy, Jr.

The following year she attended the July 13, 1991 wedding of Matthew Maxwell Kennedy and Victoria Anne Strauss in Philadelphia. Matthew is the son of assassinated Senator Robert Kennedy.

In 2013 Richard Higbie, a senior criminal investigator at the Bureau of Diplomatic Security, and Aurelia Fedenisn is a State Department whistleblower revealed a cover-up of prostitution, pedophilia and drug dealing under then Secretary of State Hillary Clinton during the Obama-Biden administration. Higbie went on record and said that the person who interfered with the investigation and shut it down was Under Secretary Patrick Kennedy. He is the youngest of three children born to Senator Edward "Ted" Kennedy – brother of slain President John F. Kennedy.

1990

By 1990 Robert Maxwell's holdings were vast – approximately 800 companies with names that seemed similar to one another. Ghislaine, who began working for him in one capacity or another as early as 1973 when she was photographed at her father's office at a computer continued at his side doing his bidding until his final days. An interesting sidenote is Robert Maxwell's introduction of computers at his offices decades before it became commonplace.

On November 5, 1990 Ghislaine flew to New York from London (by Concorde) with an envelope containing shares of the language school Berlitz, owned by Maxwell's publicly listed company. There were nine forged certificates and were part of her father's plunder from shareholders. She returned to the Mirror Group headquarters with another envelope for her father which was part of his Berlitz school plunder. The article this information is linked to states Ghislaine might have unknowingly become enmeshed in a plot initiated by her father. This author does not agree with that assessment. Ghislaine was close to 30 and had been a chip of her father's old block from the time she was a young child. While her brothers Kevin and Ian were charged with this specific fraud, Ghislaine miraculously escaped scrutiny or very likely her brothers may have refused to implicate her.

Upon Maxwell's death in 1991 it was learned that Ghislaine had been receiving an income of £100,000 – the equivalent of approximately US $130,000. When the employees of Robert Maxwell heard about the staggering amount, which they felt was unjustified, it raised eyebrows. In one of the many articles written after his death one of his employees was quoted as saying, "Nobody at the Christmas party on Friday night could remember seeing Ms. Maxwell in the office more than once – sometime in the summer of 1990."

Her title, it was discovered, was "fashion director".

FOURTEEN

Governor Bill Clinton & Mena Airport

———————

By the time he became President in 1992, Bill Clinton, the Democratic Governor of Arkansas, who'd begun his career as Attorney General of Arkansas in 1976, was already well versed in scandal. He'd been accused of rape, was said by his brother,

Roger to "have a nose like a vacuum cleaner" (referring to a cocaine habit), and had been in charge of the controversial airbase in Mena, Arkansas set up by Oliver North and the CIA.

In the 1980s Mena was used to bring in planeload after planeload of cocaine. The drugs would be sold on the streets of the United States with the proceeds used to buy weapons for the Contras. One of the pilots was Barry Seal whose life was sanitized for movie *American Made* starring Tom Cruise.

The term 'contra' is short for 'a contra-revolucion' – the counter-revolution. The Contras were various right-wing rebel groups that were backed by the United States during 1979 through the early 1990s. They fought in opposition to the socialist Sandinista Junta of National Reconstruction Government in Nicaragua. It was a covert act on the part of the U.S. who provided the rebels with both financial and military support. During President Ronald Reagan's administration, the Iran-Contra affair was exposed to the public and there were Congressional hearings making these activities on the part of the U.S. illegal. However, even after Congress vetoed continued support, the CIA continued their activities.

William Jefferson Blythe Jr. is Bill Clinton's real father. Blythe was married five times. On September 4,

1945 Blythe bigamously married Virginia Dell Cassidy – Bill's mother whom he met in Shreveport, Louisiana. Blythe died three months before Bill was born. Cassidy married Roger Clinton Sr and Bill took his name. Bill Clinton boasted of having had sex with 2,000 while in high school. He is quoted as saying that he and Hillary had to have a baby so they could appear to the public to be a "normal couple". One of his friends in Arkansas stated, "Everyone who knows him says he is the most charming man they've ever met and a man not 'bound by the truth'".

Gennifer Flowers

As the Governor of Arkansas, he had a well-known reputation as a womanizer, even after he got married. Right before the New Hampshire primary, news about his 12-year sexual relationship with Gennifer Flowers broke. Flowers had worked for the state of Arkansas and was a former cabaret dancer. Their relationship began in 1977 – a short two years after Clinton married Hillary Rodham. Bill told her he couldn't have children and she took that as a cue that she didn't have to worry about birth control. Flowers became pregnant almost immediately and believed he would leave his wife and marry her. Instead the first words out of his mouth were,

"Well, you know I will pay for an abortion." Three years later, in 1980, Hillary gave birth to their daughter Chelsea. During one of the many interviews Gennifer Flowers gave, she claims that Hillary absolutely knew about the alleged affair as soon as it began.

In Gennifer Flower's book *Passion and Betrayal* she describes how she and Bill used to play sex games with food. In what sounds like scenes right out of the film *9 ½ Week's* starring Mickey Rourke and Kim Basinger, she writes:

"Bill would slowly squeeze the honey all over my body, then sensually rub it all over me. We also used to love to sit on the floor and play sex games using all sorts of food. He would blindfold me, then go into the kitchen...I loved it when he would slowly pour juice into my mouth until it overflowed, and little streams of liquid would trickle down my naked body. Before long we'd both be so turned on, he'd be rubbing the smooth, gooey mixture all over me. He'd take me to the bed, I'd pull him down on top of me, and we'd make love. What a sensation! After those food fests we'd both be covered with ketchup and milk and whatever."

Flowers also claims they enjoyed bondage, spanking, ice cubes, and dripping wax on each other. Her nickname for Bill's penis was "Willard" and Flowers alleges that Bill would refer to Hillary as "Sarge" or "Hilla the Hun".

She writes about tying Bill Clinton up with silk scarfs to her bedposts and using a dildo vibrator on him. "I teased and played with him until he was almost out of his mind with excitement. Bill, as always, wanted to take it a step further, so the next time I tied him to the bed, he asked me to use a dildo-shaped vibrator on him. It was exciting to see him getting so aroused, and I couldn't wait to untie him so he could use it on me."

Dan Lasater

One of Clinton's best friends was Dan Lasater, an Arkansas native who grew up in poverty. At 19 Lasater started his own hamburger chain in Indiana. Once it became a success, he sold it and moved back to Arkansas where he began The Ponderosa Steakhouse chain. He also pursued his love of racing horses and the story about how Lasater met Bill Clinton changes depending on who you talk to. In one version of the story Clinton's mother and his brother Roger met him at the Oaklawn Park horseracing track because their boxes at the track were adjacent to each other. In this version Bill Clinton and his mother asked Lasater to give Roger a job since he wasn't doing well whereupon he hired him to work for one of his horse stables in Florida

However, a confidential FBI document states the meeting happened differently. According to the document, Lasater told federal agents he met Roger Clinton in 1981 when he was playing in a band and took him on as a stable hand in Florida only after he was asked to give him a job by Bill Clinton.

Lasater was a smooth talking, wheeler dealer, who owned a Rolls Royce, a private airplane, and had access to unlimited free cocaine. The free-flowing cocaine happened to have coincided with Barry Seal's undercover CIA operation in Mena, Arkansas. It also happened at the same time as the gubernatorial reign of Bill Clinton.

Roger Clinton didn't fare very well in Florida and was soon in debt to drug dealers to the tune of eight thousand dollars. Fearing for his family's safety he confided in Lasater and asked him for a loan. After he was arrested on cocaine charges and when on the witness stand in a related trial in February 1985 Roger confirmed he worked at Lasater's horse stables and that he got an $8,000 loan from him to pay off a drug dealer. He paid the dealer $4,000 and kept the other half for himself.

Lasater would go on to say that both he and Bill Clinton would provide free cocaine to young high school girls at "parties," but that Roger was the only one who participated in the sale of cocaine for profit. Lasater admitted he provided cocaine to his employees and friends in an effort to control them.

Julius "Doc" DeLaughter, a former Arkansas Police Investigator in charge of the Dan Lasater case said he used cocaine as a tool for sexual favors and also for business deals and to influence people. It ultimately led to his arrest and conviction. Lasater went to jail with Bill's brother, Roger. He also makes it clear that Lasater wasn't selling cocaine – he was giving it away. "He had huge piles of cocaine in his office. Ashtray after ashtray full and they [Lasater and Clinton] would give it to young girls."

One of these girls was a 14 and a virgin when Lasater sent her to a physician and had her put on birth control pills. She lost her virginity to Lasater and by the time DeLaughter subpoenaed her during the Lasater case, she was a hooker in Lake Tahoe.

A letter written by Patty Ann Smith states she was 16 years old and a student at North Little Rick High School when she met Dan Lasater. She told the prosecutors that Lasater introduced her to cocaine and she was a virgin until two months after meeting him. "Dan Lasater was planning on using me as a prostitute to entertain his friends." At the time she met him, he was 40 years old. Smith was further threatened with death should she reveal anything. One of his cronies told her that if she ever betrayed his trust or hurt Lasater in any way she would "not see daylight to talk about it anymore." In her letter she writes that she "saw Bill Clinton several times but he was never acting like a governor when I saw him," and claims to have witnessed Clinton take cocaine on many occasions.

The friendship between Lasater, a man who enjoyed to party with young girls, and Bill grew strong. Lasater began to sponsor fundraisers for Clinton at his offices and made his airplane available for both Hillary and Bill to use either for their fundraising activities or for their personal use. By 1983 when Bill Clinton once again became the Governor of Arkansas, Lasater owned a bond firm. He became the official underwriter with the Arkansas Development Finance Authority (DFA) for state issued bonds. Clinton awarded Lasater a $30 million bond to install a new police radio for the Arkansas State Police. During this time Lasater was under investigation for drugs. He was investigated for narcotics trafficking. Intelligence reports show a file was opened in 1983.

~

Clinton, as Governor, signed off on an undercover police sting in 1984 where both Lasater and his brother Roger was arrested on cocaine charges.

After Lasater was indicted, DeLaughter claims he was receiving "quite a bit of harassment from his department", namely, the Arkansas State Police. "I knew the reason behind this was the affiliation between the State Police and the Governor's office with Dan Lasater and his business associates."

Once Dan Lasater was convicted, he went to a minimum-security prison, a "holiday hotel", DeLaughter called it stating he only "spent six to eight months." He added, "One day after he got out, unbeknownst to anybody, Bill Clinton gave him a full and complete pardon."

Barry Seal & MENA

On August 23, 1987 Kevin Ives, 17, and Don Henry 16, were found dead on railroad tracks near Mena. Two police officers in the rural community just south of Little Rock, Arkansas were alleged to have murdered the two teenage boys after they witnessed a police-protected drug drop. The deaths were ruled an accident by Dr. Fahmy Malak, a Clinton appointed state medical examiner.

During the 1980s Mena was part of the largest drug smuggling operations in what would later become known as the Iran-Contra scandal. Barry Seal's name is synonymous with Mena, Arkansas and was said to have been connected, post-mortem, with the drug drop the murdered boys witnessed. It was Seal's route. Just because he had been killed execution style on February 19, 1986 didn't mean the drugs and guns for the Nicaraguan Contras stopped flowing.

In 1981 Russell Welsh, a criminal investigator in the Arkansas State Police, was the second investigator placed in Mena to monitor drug traffic. The first investigation began in 1977. Welsh stated "Barry Seal wasn't the first show to come to Mena and he wasn't the last."

Adler "Barry" Seal, was a former TWA pilot. He went into the drug smuggling business with the CIA in the 1970's illegally bringing first marijuana and then cocaine into the United States - in ever increasing quantities. On his Wikipedia page, it states that Seal was a "major drug smuggler for the Medellin Cartel". What is omitted is that the Medellin cartel was working with the CIA under President Ronald Reagan, then President George H.W. Bush, and later President Bill Clinton. In Arkansas, Seal was well known to both Dan Lasater and to Governor Clinton. In the book *Crossfire* by L.D. Brown Seal is described as "an overweight, jovial, almost slap-happy man." Brown, a former Arkansas

State Police trooper and Clinton's favorite bodyguard wrote in his book:

"Seal reached back to open the duffel bag in the back. He removed a manila envelope identical to the one he had given me after the first trip. I knew what was in the envelope but there was something else. He reached deeper in the bag and gave me the shock of my life. Seal's face had a sly, smirky, almost proud look as he removed a waxed paper-wrapped taped brick-shaped package from the bag. I immediately recognized it as identical to bricks of cocaine from my days in narcotics. I didn't know what to think and began demanding to know what was going on. I cursed, ranted and raved and I believe I actually caused Seal to wonder if I might pull a gun and arrest him. Seal threw up his hands and tried to calm me down saying everything was all right and quickly exited my car. He removed the bag from the bag and hustled back toward the plane. I at once felt a sense of panic and relief that Seal was gone. Had he left something in the car? Was I about to be surrounded by the police? Wait a minute I was the police and furthermore this was an operation sanctioned by the C.I.A and I was recruited by them - and by Bill Clinton. [...] I would become furious with Bill for shepherding me through this mess, indeed for getting me involved."

The parents of the boys refused to accept that they had died of an accident and pressed for a new investigation. A new autopsy on the teenagers was performed. It was determined that by the time the train hit them, one of the boys was already dead and the other unconscious. Don had been stabbed in the back and Kevin's skull had been crushed before the train ran over their bodies. Their deaths were reclassified as homicides.

Linda Ives, Kevin's mother maintained a website for years hoping for someone to be indicted for the murder and subsequent murder of the boys. The website disappeared just before Jeffrey Epstein's arrest in 2019. I was able to find one of the pages. It read:

"August 23, 1987, in a rural community just south of Little Rock, police officers murdered two teenage boys because they witnessed a police-protected drug drop. The drop was part of a drug smuggling operation based at a small airport in Mena, Arkansas. The Mena operation was set up in the early 1980's by the notorious drug smuggler, Barry Seal. Facing prison after a drug conviction in Florida, Seal flew to Washington, D.C., where he put together a deal that allowed him to avoid prison by becoming an informant for the government. As a government informant against drug smugglers, Seal testified he worked for the CIA and the DEA. In one federal court case, he testified that his income from

March 1984 to August 1985, was between $700,000 and $800,000. This period was AFTER making his deal with the government. Seal testified that nearly $600,000 of this came from smuggling drugs while working for -- and with the permission of the DEA. In addition to his duties as an informant, Seal was used by CIA operatives to help finance the Nicaraguan Contras. The CIA connection to the Mena operation was undeniable when a cargo plane given to Seal by the CIA was shot down over Nicaragua with a load of weapons. In spite of the evidence, every investigator who has tried to expose the crimes of Mena has been professionally destroyed, and those involved in drug smuggling operations have received continued protection from state and federal authorities."

On her original website she wrote "the internet would be the demise of the cover-up". And added: "It is getting harder for the mainstream media to ignore the obvious."

Bill Clinton runs for President

Bill Clinton announced his presidential run in 1991. By then allegations of his sexual trysts with multiple women were undermining his candidacy. Betsey Ross Wright served as chief of staff to Governor Clinton for seven years. She admitted she had been hired to go after 26 women and conduct character assassinations on each one. However, if Bill wanted to win, it was decided that Hillary would have to address the public. An interview with 60 Minutes was arranged.

On January 26, 1992 right after the Super Bowl the 60 Minutes interview with Bill and Hillary Clinton aired. Bill Clinton told the show's host, Steve Kroft, that he'd spoken to Gennifer only two times. He claimed he had never been to her condominium, and denied ever having an affair with her. Clinton emphasized he and Hillary were not in an arranged marriage. It was a marriage based on love he proclaimed looking straight into the camera. In 1978 Bill had bragged to his close aide, Arkansas state trooper Roger Perry, that "Gennifer could suck a tennis ball through a garden hose."

Gary Johnson was the next-door neighbor of Gennifer Flowers in the Qaupaw Towers apartment building in Little Rock, Arkansas. He had a security video camera over his apartment door. The camera also caught images of whoever came in and out of Flowers' apartment. He had a lot of evidence in the videos showing Clinton entering her apartment for years during his time as governor and while married to Hillary.

Just two weeks before the Democratic National Convention, on June 26, 1992 Gary Johnson was on the floor of his apartment beaten and left for dead. He claimed "three big, beefy men with crew cuts looked like Arkansas state troopers" had asked him for the videotapes of Clinton entering Flowers' apartment. After handing them over the men beat him. They broke his elbows, his collar bones, ruptured his spleen and his bladder with holes the size of half dollars and crushed his nose and sinus cavities.

FIFTEEN

Conchita Sarnoff & Victor Ostrovsky

I was doing some basic research trying to connect with Conchita Sarnoff who had written about the Jeffrey Epstein and Ghislaine Maxwell case before anyone else. In 2010 Sarnoff had six articles published in *The Daily Beast* after claiming all other mainstream media had rejected her.

The first thing I discovered was there was no way to contact her. Her social profile had almost disappeared.

No twitter.

No Instagram.

No Facebook.

Furthermore, the information listed on her LinkedIn page – went nowhere. Her non-profit website to help trafficked children *Alliance to Rescue Victims of Trafficking* (ATRVT) had been replaced with a 'Coming Soon' page. Another website was non-functioning. And emails I sent her were returned as "undeliverable". However, the non-profit anti-trafficking website used to be there with all sorts of information about who sat on the Board of Directors – and it's archived. More on this shortly.

I wasn't sure what this meant. Was Sarnoff threatened and gone "underground" to avoid being killed? I didn't know. It could have meant anything. It seemed odd. She had appeared on almost every outlet – mainstream television and indie podcasts promoting a book she wrote on Jeffrey Epstein called *TrafficKing*.

I pressed on and decided to listen to her older podcasts. In the interviews Sarnoff claims she had become obsessed with the Epstein case. That it changed the trajectory of her life. It made her want to help trafficked children.

She went on to add that she had met Jeffrey Epstein at his home in the 1990s. He wasn't very well educated she confided. She said met and befriended Ghislaine Maxwell – afterwards. Meeting them separately before they became a couple in the 1990s. She repeated she met them separately – Epstein being first, Maxwell later before they met each other.

Sarnoff also gave the now tired line that Ghislaine was devastated after the death of her father and Epstein took his place. She was very flattering of Ghislaine Maxwell stating she was very well educated and vivacious. Then added they all ran in the same circles and had similar friends.

When Sarnoff mentioned in her interviews that her book *TrafficKing* had been published by Victor Ostrovsky I sat up and took notice. Something seemed off and I began to dig.

Victor Ostrovsky is a former Mossad agent.

Moreover, he wasn't just an agent – he was one of the top men in Israel's Mossad. Ostrovsky knew Robert Maxwell and has acknowledged that Mossad was financing many of its operations in Europe using the money stolen from Maxwell's newspaper pension fund. They got their hands on the funds almost as soon as Maxwell made the purchase of the Mirror Newspaper Group with money lent to him by Mossad.

I needed to dig deeper and needed to see how Mossad operative Victor Ostrovsky "published" her book. It didn't take a long time to get this information. The inside of her book lists a company named zumbaba.com as her publisher. I discovered the domain name is owned by Victor Ostrovsky. As is the website page with that name and the Facebook page it connects to. Problem is – these is nothing behind these single internet pages. There are no other authors. No other books. No followers to speak of on the *"Publishing Company's"* Facebook page. Both appear to be fronts—with no substantive information. Just what a Mossad agent would need.

It gets weirder. The attorney for her non-profit is Tefft W. Smith who works at Kirkland & Ellis. If that sounds familiar to you, it's because that is the firm where Jeffrey Epstein's attorneys came from. Jay Lefkowitz, Kenneth Starr – even Alexander Acosta and former Attorney General William "Bill" Barr.

Tefft Smith's bio on their website reads:

"Tefft was selected as a civilian participant for the "capstone" National Security Seminar week of the Army War College's year long program for future military leaders. He was invited to participate in the Naval War College's similar program. Tefft has long been a nationally ranked squash player, having won 5 National

Age Group Championships, currently ranked #1 in his age bracket. He has a Sports Car Club of America car racing license.

Tefft has been and is active on many Pro Bono matters. He authored a book for the Due process of Law Foundation, which promotes enhancing the rule of law in South America and elsewhere, entitled 'Selecting the Best, the Selection of High-Level Judges in the United States, Europe and Asia. Tefft helped form and is counsel to the Alliance to Rescue the Victims of Sex Trafficking."

Why would a non-profit to help trafficked children be represented by a law firm that is notorious for having defended the most prolific pedophile of our time?

Who is Conchita Sarnoff?

While I don't want this to become a biography on Conchita Sarnoff – it's important to note that she married into a family of spies. In May of 1984 Conchita Maria Suarez, the daughter of Pedro Suarez Hernandez and Conchita Priete Suarez of Asturias and Granada, Spain, married Daniel Jay Sarnoff.

Daniel is the eldest son of Thomas Sarnoff and the grandson of David Sarnoff. David was best friends with CIA Director Allen Dulles and together they created

Radio Free Europe which became a large part of the technological core of the NSA. During the war, David's son Robert worked in the broadcast arm of the Office of Strategic Services (OSS), the precursor of the CIA.

Robert was the President of RCA—NBC's parent company. David remained its chairman until his death in 1970. Another interesting note is that David Sarnoff owned a mansion at 44 East 71st Street in Manhattan. The house is on the very same street as Jeffrey Epstein's mansion located at 9 East 71st Street—although it should be noted Sarnoff sold the property two decades before Epstein moved to the block. The property is now the Korean Consulate.

With all of these legitimate mainstream media connections – it seems implausible that Conchita Sarnoff, as she repeatedly claimed, could get "no mainstream media" interested in her story on Jeffrey Epstein.

What she does brilliantly is attack anyone else's work on Jeffrey Epstein and Ghislaine Maxwell. She has attacked James Patterson's work. Anyone who has written anything on Epstein or Maxwell – she has something negative to say about that person. One is left believing that perhaps this woman - this Conchita Sarnoff is the ultimate expert on Jeffrey Epstein. The second thing she does is blame everything on Bill Clinton and vigorously defends Donald Trump.

But, wait, there's more.

Board of Directors

Among the interesting people that sit on the Board of Directors are the following:

Under Secretary of State for Global Affairs Paula J. Dobriansky who was nominated by President George W. Bush on March 12, 2001 and became Under Secretary of State for Global Affairs. From 1997-2001 Ambassador Dobriansky served as Senior Vice President and Director of the Washington Office of the Council on Foreign Relations.

Jeffrey Epstein was a member from 1995 until 2009 and undoubtedly they knew each other. Dobriansky serves on the Defense Policy Board, the Secretary of State's Foreign Affairs Policy Board, and the EXIM Advisory Committee, serving as Chair of the Subcommittee on Strategic Competition with China.

Otto Juan Reich (born 1944 or 1945) is an American diplomat and lobbyist who worked in the administrations of Presidents Ronald Reagan, George H.W. Bush, and George W. Bush. He has been dubbed a "political thug" who is "eternally implicated in secret CIA networks".

From 1983 to 1986, Reich established and managed the inter-agency Office of Public Diplomacy for Latin American and the Caribbean (OPD), which sought to promote the Contra guerrillas in Nicaragua. He managed a staff including officials from the Central Intelligence Agency (CIA) and The Pentagon, some of whom were personnel trained in psychological warfare. Reich reported to Oliver North, who then worked at the National Security Council (NSC), although the office itself was under the State Department which is always code for the CIA.

Everything I've discovered is purely circumstantial evidence. It could mean nothing or it could mean she's a spy. In the world of Jeffrey Epstein and Ghislaine Maxwell anything seems plausible.

SIXTEEN

The New York Daily News

———————

On a cold and cloudy morning in mid-March 1991 Robert Maxwell, his daughter Ghislaine, his secretary, and a small entourage tucked themselves into rented black stretch limousines and made their way through New York traffic to the headquarters of the New York Daily News on 42nd Street between Second and Third Avenues. To passersby the black limousines, one after the other, looked like they were part of a funeral procession.

Maxwell's yacht, the *Lady Ghislaine,* was docked less than three blocks away near the United Nations where he always moored her when in the city. He had now been visiting New York for close to forty years. However, his yacht had only been in his possession since 1986.

He had become more like a rock star than a businessman and was accustomed to traveling without a group of yes-men. Some likened it to him behaving like a politician. His entourage knew to trail close behind so as to ensure his every whim was catered to. None of them ever knew which side of him they were on. His good or his bad. He was known for being unpredictable and hyperactive working 18-hour days seven days every week. One day Bob had fired one of his own sons, Ian, because he showed up late to a meeting.

On Bob's part he thought of most people as being less than human. Even people of distinction he routinely dismissed as a "bunch of arseholes". Not everyone fell for his ruse, however, among them Princess Diana who referred to him as "that odious man" and Nancy Reagan who squirmed when she saw his rotund figure barreling through the corridors of the White House.

Two days earlier *The New York Times* wrote that he was worth $2 billion and was among the U.K.'s wealthiest men. Within the last several years his holdings via Maxwell Communications Corporation had made it more of an American business than a British one. However, they added that his debts exceeded $3.2 billion. Investors had begun to worry and analysts weighed in and stated that his next large repayment to his bankers was not due until 1992. Angela Bawtree, an analyst for Warburg Securities in London said, "He's not facing any imminent cash squeeze."

His plan was to fire 800 workers which would cut costs by $70 million per year. But his larger plan was he wanted to become a household name in the United States. Just as he had done in the U.K.

The limousines pulled up beside a newsstand on East 42nd street and came to a stop. The cars began to pile up behind them.

Robert Maxwell stepped out of the car. Despite his large size he moved quickly like a cheetah chasing his prey. His large black wingtip shoes stomped like King Kong one heavy foot first and then the other whereupon they landed onto the sidewalk. He wore a camel hair coat and a striking red bow tie. A green and white striped cap was perched on his head. He took in the crowd. About 300 people and several tv crews with their cameras were lined up to gawk at the man who was said to be saving the ailing newspaper.

He took off his cap revealing pitch-black hair which contrasted sharply with his pale and flaccid skin. Layers of sagging skin drooped under his chin and onto the collar of his starched white shirt. He smiled radiantly as he twirled his hat and held up the other hand for silence.

Ghislaine, standing next to him, smiled graciously as the cameras popped like fireworks one right after the other. She seemed like a stick figure – rail thin like Audrey Hepburn – next to his very large, very round frame. When asked by people how she stayed so thin her reply was, "I do it the way Nazis did it with the Jews, the Auschwitz diet. I just don't eat".

Her thick black hair fell just above her shoulders. And her signature bangs were parted three-quarters of the way covering most her forehead. The inch long earrings she wore swung back and her head moved from her father to the crowd. Despite the honking horns, sirens, the loud screeching of the buses, and the constant hammering of new construction that filled the air, she only heard him.

"This is a great day. A great day for me, but above all for New York," Maxwell announced in a deep booming voice. "It's the first good thing that New

Yorkers have seen happen in a long while. The city has lost confidence in itself. People are departing. I say enough! New York still has something to say. The fact that I have chosen New York is a vote of tremendous confidence in this city."

He then held both his arms over his head, his fists clenched in triumph. "It's a miracle! A Miracle on 42nd Street!"

Ghislaine had a role in New York. Her father created a spot for her at the Daily News. She was to be in charge of "special projects". No doubt he would continue to send her to celebrity weddings and events in order to report back on the information she was able to collect. "Information is power," he'd drilled into her since she was a young girl.

Traveling back and forth from London to New York took less than three hours on the Concorde. She was too fond of her spacious London home not to want to spend some of her time there. But she loved the non-stop energy of this city almost as much as her father did. The social life among the old and new money set was just her speed. It reminded her of her days at Oxford when she would return to school after an all-night party at the exclusive Annabel's or Tramp.

She was already close friends with Ivana, Donald Trump's wife. Ivana was born in Czechoslovakia just like her father and she bonded with her as they exchanged stories. On Ghislaine's part she told her how her father, a Czech immigrant refugee named Jan Hoch, transformed himself into a publishing mogul. On Ivana's part she explained that in 1971 she married an Austrian skier named Alfred Winklmayr in an arranged marriage. After their ceremony her new husband returned to Vienna while she waited for her Austrian passport to arrive. The newlyweds then moved to Canada where they remained married for two years before dissolving the sham marriage. "He was a friend," Ivana always added in her thick accent.

Although Ivana was locked in a bitter divorce battle with her husband, Donald Trump over the new woman in his life, Marla Maples, she was friendly with him too. He was going to be attending the party later that evening on *The Lady Ghislaine*. Her father had known him for years – both sharing some of the same attorneys, public relations people, political connections and business associates.

The *New York Daily News* was the oldest and most iconic newspaper in the United States. At its height, in 1947, it sold 2.4 million copies a day and 4.7 million on Sunday. The tabloid was founded by Joseph Medill Patterson, a millionaire, whose mother was the daughter of the founder of the Chicago Tribune and who later became the Mayor of Chicago. It was launched on June 24, 1919 and had immediate success.

However, due to a series of problems with the unions by February 1991 the paper was a thin 20 pages and circulation dropped to shy of 300,000 people.

New Yorkers were losing their favorite newspaper that featured photos, cartoons, sports and gory mobster slayings on its front cover. Instead of society figures, the New York Daily News ran regular stories on underground figures like Vincent 'the Chin' Gigante, boss of the Genovese crime family and John Gotti, head of the Gambino family.

The newspaper editor Jim Hoge was a Washington, D.C. correspondent in the 1960s and has been a member of the Council of Foreign Affairs for decades. He was appointed president and publisher of the New York Daily News in 1984.

Of note, Hoge left the New York Daily News when Maxwell took over and today works as a senior advisor at Teneo Intelligence – the PR firm founded by former President Bill Clinton's deputy assistant, Doug Band. In 2011 it was announced that Tony Blair, former Prime Minister of the United Kingdom and Bill Clinton were members of Teneo's advisory board. Clinton was paid $2.5 million per year for his role.

In 1989 Hoge decided to take on the mafia and the labor unions which they controlled. They were draining the paper of their profits. To do this he used non-union labor and hired out of town journalists. He went as far as renting a warehouse in New Jersey. There he built a replica of the New York office for his writers to work to keep them away from the office in the city which was under attack by the mob. Hoge even began using non-union delivery trucks.

The Mafia wasn't happy. In addition to skimming profits from sale of the newspaper they had become accustomed to using the delivery vans to delivery drugs to the other boroughs.

As security for his team in New Jersey he surrounded the property with a chain-link fence with barbed wire, hired security guards with large German shepherd dogs who patrolled the premises around the clock.

The *Chicago Tribune* which owned the *New York Daily News* decided enough was enough and began to see if they could sell the troubled newspaper now worth pennies on the dollar.

Maxwell worked out a deal with the unions. There was even speculation that they paid him to take the newspaper off their hands. None of the troubles with the unions bothered Robert Maxwell. He knew how to deal with members of organized crime. Uppermost on his mind was how his arch enemy, Rupert Murdoch, would react when he heard the news that he now owned the *New York Daily News*.

≈

As Maxwell was about the launch into another self-congratulatory speech two police officers haltingly approached him.

In a respectful tone, uncommon for New York City cops, they asked him to please move the limousines as traffic had begun to pile up.

Maxwell smiled at the police officers and thanked them effusively for their help.

Then, with a look of triumph, he began marching up the street as if he were the ringmaster of a parade, his coat flapping in the wind behind him. Ghislaine, along with their dutiful entourage, followed with the cheering crowd at their heels. Robert Maxwell was the hero of the hour—the true savior of the *Daily News*. Or, at least, that is how it seemed. The stretch limousines began to inch their way back into the traffic and disappeared. They would return when summoned.

Ghislaine stepped into the lobby of the 36-story Art Deco landmark building that now belonged to her for the first time. They all piled into different elevators and emerged on the floor where Jim Hoge's and her father's offices were located.

The secretary dutifully laid Maxwell's briefcase on the large desk. Ghislaine's eyes were scanning the room and she noticed it was smaller than Hoge's office.

"Why is your office smaller than Jim Hoge's?" She asked her father who had just sunk with a groan into the large leather chair.

"Is it?" he asked his eyebrows forming a V-shape. "I didn't notice, but I shall get that fixed in short order." He loved how she looked after him. But he wasn't going to praise her otherwise it would cost him another wild spending trip.

Jim Hoge recalls that Maxwell asked him for a favor that day.

"Would you mind if I stood here with the door open and shouted at you for a while?"

After the battle with the unions and the mafia he saw no reason to decline. "Go ahead."

Maxwell began by banging his fist on his desk shouting how outrageous it was that his office was larger than his own. He went on like this for a full 40 seconds. At which point he looked him squarely in the eye and said, "Thank you" in a quieter voice before leaving the room.

Hoge soon discovered that Maxwell staged the scene to impress Ghislaine. She had been standing just outside and within earshot the whole time.

~

In an article dated March 19, 1994, now long scrubbed, entitled 'Maxwell's money laundry' written by George Garneau it cites that U.S. bankruptcy judge, Tina Brozman, found that Maxwell's reason for the purchase was for money laundering purposes. Quoting the judge's ruling, he added:

"The evidence here compels the conclusion that Maxwell's interest, both in purchasing and operating the Daily News, was to keep the newspaper alive so that Maxwell Newspapers could function as a money-laundering device," Brozman said in a scathing 23-page decision riddled with references to fraud, misappropriation of funds, deceit and self-interest."

The judge also found that Maxwell used the Daily News to secure a $78 million loan from Bankers Trust but only put into the tabloid $8.45 million. Another time, she added, "He negotiated to borrow $86 million from Bankers Trust for MGN and sent the funds off on a great circular ride through the Daily News and back to Bankers Trust to repay another loan."

In Robert Maxwell's offices on the ninth floor of what had become known as the Maxwell House in London young bankers streamed in to collect on the mounting debts he owed. His sons, Kevin and Ian, greeted each one and engaged them in conversation meant to alleviate their fears. Many of these young bankers lulled by these conversations began to refer to Robert Maxwell as "Uncle".

Years later Jeffrey Epstein would also be referred to as "Uncle Jeff" by many of the younger people around him – including the offspring of Donald Trump.

It is worth sharing a story lost to history. Joseph Mengele known after the slaughter of many innocent Jews at the Auschwitz concentration camp as the 'Angel of Death' introduced himself as "Uncle Mengele" when visiting the children who were part of his sadistic human experiments. A former Auschwitz inmate doctor said of Mengele:

"He was capable of being so kind to the children, to have them become fond of him, to bring them sugar, to think of small details in their daily lives, and to do things we would genuinely admire ... And then, next to that, ... the crematoria smoke, and these children, tomorrow or in a half-hour, he is going to send them there. Well, that is where the anomaly lay."

SEVENTEEN

Donald Trump & Adnan Khashoggi

———————

Ghislaine Maxwell was onboard *The Lady Ghislaine* in 1989 when her father moored it next to the United Nations as he did whenever he was in New York City. He held his usual extravagant party with caviar flown in from Paris on the Concorde. Donald

Trump, who was then in the middle of splitting with his wife Ivana, arrived without her. He was accompanied by his attorneys, Roy Cohn and his business partner who preferred staying in the shadows: Tom Bolan.

The event was covered by several newspapers and was attended by CBS correspondent Mike Wallace who appeared regularly on *60 Minutes* and who spent his first summer after graduation working "on-air" at Interlochen Center for the Arts. It should be noted that Jeffrey Epstein attended Interlochen when he was 14 years old in 1967. A photo of him at the camp has made the rounds on social media. One of the victims in the current case against Ghislaine Maxwell was also at Interlochen when she was 13. She alleges Maxwell procured her for Epstein.

A photo of Robert Maxwell and Donald Trump at the 1989 event was salvaged from approximately 1,000 pictures found at a Florida thrift shop. They are believed to have been thrown out by Ivana. In 2014, a South Florida collector purchased the box containing a treasure trove of Trump's once private collection.

The photo shows five men standing very close locked in conversation. From left to right are Steve

Ross, Donald Trump, John Tower, Mike Wallace and Robert Maxwell. In the background is a life-size portrait of Ghislaine wearing a white sweater over a pair of jeans seated on the floor.

The social affair on Robert Maxwell's yacht received a small amount of news coverage. The following May 5, 1989 *New York Daily News* article among them. It's title: "The Donald sans shoes". It reads:

"Everybody, but everybody at the party aboard British media mogul Robert Maxwell's yacht Wednesday night had to doff off their shoes before boarding the "Lady Ghislaine". Maxwell insisted, and his guests cooperated, including Donald Trump (minus Ivana), who has a much bigger yacht and was happy to compare notes with Maxwell. There were John Tower; ex-Navy secretary John Lehman, now with PaineWebber; lawyer Tom Bolan; literary agent Mort Janklow; UN envoy Thomas Pickering; Peter Kalikow, owner of the New York Post; Maxwell's daughter, Ghislaine and his niece, Helen Atkin of Macmillan, the publishing house Maxwell recently took over. No one could tell who didn't make the final list, but we do know that Martha Smilgis of Time was disinvited by David Adler, public relations chief at Macmillan. She wrote the profile of Maxwell which he apparently did not like."

In this writer's opinion the people who attended deserve a deeper look.

Steve Ross, whose father changed their last name from Rechnitz to Ross, was the CEO of Time Warner. Steven Spielberg said of Ross, "Steve was very much what I wish my father was". He dedicated his 1993 film *Schindler's List* to Ross. Ross is credited for creating MTV in which Maxwell was also invested.

In 1977 Ross tested a cable television show named *QUBE* in Columbus, Ohio. It collected private information from viewers which was stored in their database. After watching a program it would ask viewers to identify their favorite politicians as part of a national survey. When subscribers began to express their concerns Warner assured them their information would be kept private. When privacy concerns about a family's specific interests, political views and other personal information the "*QUBE* experiment" was ended. The Church Committee hearings of 1975 exposed intelligence operations by the CIA, NSA and the FBI showed domestic spying abuses against ordinary citizens.

John Tower was a Republican United States Senator from Texas who served from 1961 to 1985. Tower also led the *Tower Commission* which investigated the Iran-

Contra affair. According to Gordon Thomas and Thomas Dillon, who co-authored the book *Robert Maxwell, Israel's Superspy,* Tower was bribed by the Mossad through Maxwell. He told Maxwell his price was $200,000 per year to provide an in to Ronald Reagan's White House. It was to be written off as a consultant's fee. For this amount he promised Maxwell he would open the doors to Capitol Hill, to defense contractors – even to the Oval office itself.

Tower allegedly colluded with Maxwell in the sale of the Mossad-bugged PROMIS software to Los Alamos laboratories in New Mexico. The town is most famous for being the birthplace of the atomic bomb. However, it is also the place where the nuclear secrets of the United States are kept and as such it is one of the most secure locations on the planet.

Tower and Maxwell liked telling crude jokes. When Strom Thurmond, who served for 48 years as a Senator, married a 22-year-old beauty queen at the age of 70 Tower publicly quipped, "When they bury Strom, they'll have to beat his pecker with a baseball bat to keep the coffin lid down."

John Tower died in a plane crash on April 5, 1991 a few months before Maxwell's death in November of the same year.

Tom Bolan is an attorney who worked alongside Roy Cohn for decades is often overlooked. However, he is as well-connected as Cohn. Bolan began his career in the 1950s as a prosecutor working as assistant U.S. attorney for the Southern District of New York (SDNY). He handled Ronald Reagan's transition team in the 1980s played a key role in the selection of major federal judicial appointments for then Senator D'Amato. One of these included former FBI agent Louis J. Freeh for the bench. In 1993 Freeh was appointed Director of the FBI by President Bill Clinton.

It's worth noting that Louis Freeh, during the time he was an attorney at the Southern District of New York (SDNY), was lead prosecutor in the 1980s case dubbed the "Pizza Connection". Pizza parlors were frequently used as fronts for drug sales by Sicilian organized crime families. The defense attorney was Ivan Fisher. He represented Salvatore Catalano, a member of the Bonanno crime family, and at the time its acting boss.

In 1992 Jeffrey Epstein rented the former Iranian Embassy from the State Department in circumstances that have never been fully explained and in 1996 sublet it to Ivan Fisher. The U.S. government sued both Epstein and Fisher claiming the sublet was illegal although Fisher claimed Epstein assured him the State Department "signed off on the deal". This author believes Epstein met Fisher during the years he was a bounty hunter working collaboratively with the Feds.

Roy Cohn and Tom Bolan allegedly had blackmail tapes on everyone. Cohn has been described as a "cheating, corrupt, tax-dodging cocaine-snorting New York lawyer linked to the Mafia pedophile who abused boys on both sides of the Atlantic". Cohn is well-known for his "blackmail parties" where young teenage boys had sex with powerful men including J. Edgar Hoover while being filmed and photographed. Cohn represented Steve Rubell and Ian Schrager co-owners of Studio 54 when they were charged with tax evasion.

Cohn began his long-term association with Donald Trump when his father, Fred, and he were accused by the Justice Department in 1973 of systematically violating the Fair Housing Act of 1968 by refusing to rent to blacks. The lawsuit allegations included evidence from black and white "testers" who had sought to rent apartments within their 39 buildings which contained over 14,000 apartments. The white testers were told of vacancies while the black testers were not. The complaint also alleged Trump employees placed codes next to housing applicants names to indicate if they were black. The lawsuit was quietly settled three years later although Trump would falsely boast they won.

Robert Maxwell had been doing business in New York since the 1950s and had become acquainted with the Trump family. By the time of the party on the *Lady Ghislaine* in 1989 Maxwell knew Trump had become interested in possibly running for President of the United States. The two men had many commonalities aside from their inflated egos and preference for red ties and baseball hats. In many ways Trump appears to have looked upon Maxwell as a mentor of sorts. Not only do they share personality traits but they also shared some of the same attorneys and public relations people. A 1989 article in *The New York Times* states Trump and Maxwell used Howard Rubenstein as their publicist.

What most people don't see is the small army of people working in the background who orchestrate the public image of powerbrokers like Robert Maxwell and Donald Trump. The PR men who toil in the background making sure that favorable articles of these men with monstrous egos, devoid of any desire for greater good, appear to the public as if that is their goal. That they *are* good men – worthy of the public's trust.

Rubinstein is one of these men and while his name is not well known – his clients are known worldwide. He has represented Adnan Khashoggi, Fred Trump, Rupert Murdoch, Charles Kushner, The New York Yankees, News Corporation (parent company of the

New York Post), Columbia University, the Metropolitan Opera and later: Jeffrey Epstein.

Rudy Giuliani referred to him as "the dean of damage control".

By the time Donald Trump was on Robert Maxwell's yacht alongside John Tower and Robert Maxwell he was already one of Jeffrey Epstein's closest friends. In the 1980s Jeffrey Epstein was introduced to one of Donald Trump and Ivana's long-term friends, Nikki Haskell.

Haskell was a fixture at the New York club *Studio 54*, the brainchild of Steve Rubell and Ian Schrager. This was hedonism unleashed. A place where men could wear a loincloth and women could wear nothing at all. Where cocaine was on the menu and couples and groups had sex in the open. In 1978 when the famed nightclub was raided by federal agents Roy Cohn was hired to represent them. Cohn had been the attorney for Ian Schrager's father, Max the Jew – a powerful New York mob figure. The FBI were seeking evidence of organized crime involvement in the club which was a nightly gathering spot for some of the world's most famous, wealthy and influential people.

Haskell is 14 years older than Jeffrey Epstein having turned 80 recently. She is named as one of Epstein's first "notable dates". In an article by the *Mail on Sunday* dated November 15, 1992 'The mystery of Ghislaine Maxwell's secret love' they write :

"Epstein's social rise has been accompanied by a remorseless attraction to well-connected, rich and beautiful women. One of his first notable dates was Nikki Haskel, a former TV talk-show hostess who met him six years ago. Haskell was giving some of the most prominent parties in New York, and Epstein, who lived close by became a regular guest. "Jeffrey didn't talk about his past, although he claimed to be a concert pianist," she said last week.

"She experienced Epstein's love of intrigue. "He told me he was a spy hired by corporations to find major amounts of money which had been embezzled," she says. "He made it sound very exciting and glamorous. "Epstein escorted Haskell to the annual BEST Awards in New York, a meretricious event celebrating the best dressed people in America. Haskell said: "In the middle, Jeffrey got up and said 'I have to go'. When I asked why, he said: "Just look at me as a doctor who has to make a house call. "Who was he meeting at midnight on a Saturday?"

Adnan Khashoggi

In 1972 *The Godfather*—a movie based on Mario Puzzo's best-selling book about a fictional Mafia family headed by Vito Corleone in New York City received critical acclaim. Parts of the film are based on the *Five Families* in the Mafia in New York. The character of Johnny Fortane was based on the singer Frank Sinatra and Moe Greene on Frank Costello – the crime boss of the Luciano crime family. His associates included Meyer Lansky, Benjamin "Bugsy" Siegel, Vito Genovese and Tommy "Three-Finger Brown" Lucchese. Marlon Brando's character was a composite of Frank Costello and Carlo Gambino – two real life crime bosses.

Al Pacino portrays his youngest son, Michael Corleone, and Diane Keaton plays the part of his girlfriend, Kay Adams, who later becomes his second wife. The scene where Pacino and Keaton go Christmas shopping was filmed at Best & Co on Fifth Avenue in New York City.

Best & Co was owned by Meshulam Riklis through one of his company's McCrory's which also operated Lerner Shops and S. Klein Department Stores. Riklis was known in the 1980s as the "junk bond king" who taught Michael Milken of Drexel, Burnham & Lambert the ropes; and was among his first clients. In 1985 Riklis sold Lerner Shops to Leslie Wexner. The story of the Best & Co building would later play a role in how he built Trump Tower. As an example he purchased the air rights over the famed Tiffany's allowing him to build a larger and taller building.

George Ross a real estate attorney became Donald Trump's attorney in 1980. Prior to this he represented his father, Fred Trump, Leona Helmsley, Sam LeFrak, Bill Zeckendorf, Sol Goldman and other well-known New York developers. Ross also appeared as one of two advisors in Trump's hit TV series *The Apprentice* and in 2005 wrote a book, *Trump Strategies for Real Estate: Billionaire Lessons for the Small Investor.*

In the book he explains how he helped Arthur Cohen build Olympic Towers – a 51-story building just north of St. Patrick's Cathedral between 51st and 52nd Streets. Cohen, at the time, was a real estate developer whose holdings included Hotel Pennsylvania, formerly known as the Statler hotel (where CIA scientist Frank Olson was said to have jumped or fallen to his death from the 10th floor in November 28, 1953. The United States government first described his death as a suicide and later an accident. His family alleges he was murdered because he was about to talk about his role in the MK-Ultra program). Arthur Cohen later partnered with Ian Schrager of Studio 54 fame to build a string of boutique hotels.

The piece of property Cohen wanted to use on Fifth Avenue consisted of two parcels. One owned by Aristotle Onassis where he kept his flagship store for Olympic Airways and the air rights owned by Meshulam Riklis's McCrory's where Best & Co was located.

Cohen who became one of Riklis's close friends convinced him to sell him the building instead of just the air rights. Onassis also agreed to sell him the building.

There was, however, one problem. Both Onassis and Riklis wanted to rent the top floors of the new building as part of the deal. "Onassis's ego," Ross wrote in his book, "would not tolerate his offices being lower than Riklis."

Ross solved this problem by having the men rent alternating floors. Onassis got the top floor followed by Riklis with the next floor given to Onassis and then the following one to Riklis and so on.

Olympic Tower was completed in 1976. In addition to Aristotle Onassis and Meshulam Riklis it also became home to Adnan Khashoggi. Khashoggi paid $1.45 million for the 45th and 47th floors. The 12-room duplex had five bedrooms, a ballroom, a sauna, a chef's kitchen large enough to serve 300 people and a 16-foot swimming pool. Khashoggi is the uncle of Dodi Al-Fayed, who died in a fatal car crash with Princess Diana in Paris in 1997.

Adnan Khashoggi was an arms dealer. A successful one. In the 1980s he was among the world's wealthiest men estimated to be worth $4 billion. His deals were not made in dark dungy rooms but in parties aboard his yacht, the 'Nabila' where he entertained his guests with champagne, caviar, Hollywood A-listers and a string of young beautiful girls. One of these girls, Pamela Bordes, gave interviews claiming to be part of his sex trafficking and prostitution ring. She said, "I went everywhere, did everything, I was a sexual bait or a sexual bribe or a sexual present".

Donald Trump told Ronald Kessler, Khashoggi's biographer, "Khashoggi understood the art of bringing people together and putting together a deal better than almost anyone – all the bullshitting part of talk and entertainment."

Trump purchased Khashoggi's yacht, *Nabila* named after his daughter from the Sultan of Brunei in 1986. It had a 12-seat movie theatre, a swimming pool, two saunas, a disco, a billiard room, a jacuzzi, a three-chair hair salon, a patisserie, and 11 guest rooms all decorated in white chamois leather and white plush carpeting throughout the five decks. The master suite had four rooms with a solid gold sink in the bathroom. There was also an on-board hospital and a private room for a morgue.

The ship was used for a Bond film, *Never Say Never Again*. It was also equipped with 150 telephones and a satellite communications system used to arrange commodities trades and arms deals. This allowed Khashoggi to slip the yacht into international waters, where sovereign restrictions on business transactions do not apply. The yacht also had a helicopter landing pad.

Stories still float around recounting the extraordinary parties Khashoggi held on the yacht with dozens of beautiful young girls he used to close his deals. Told less frequently are the details of the many hidden cameras in the bedrooms and elsewhere in the event the perks were not enough. Blackmail, it seems, was one of the many weapons at his disposal.

Adnan Khashoggi is said to have entertained five heads of state, including three kings simultaneously on the yacht.

In 1987 when Khashoggi defaulted on a loan having used the yacht as collateral Donald Trump purchased it and renamed her *Trump Princess*.

When Robert Maxwell purchased *The Daily News* he bankrolled *Maxwell Corporate Gifts* as a business for Ghislaine to own and run. It is likely this too was a front as its clear all businesses owned by Robert Maxwell were actually an arm of his intelligence gathering operation.

"I'd like to sell some of the gifts to Donald Trump," Ghislaine began while still at the office before they heading out for the evening.

"Why the fuck would Donald Trump want to waste time seeing you with your crappy gifts when he has a multi-million-dollar business to run?"

Maxwell's former secretary Carol Bragoli said, "Maxwell would expect everyone he knew in business to buy them off her so she didn't have to go out and sell it. She just had to say whose daughter she was and they sold themselves."

EIGHTEEN

A Spy Exposed

Less than one month before his ghastly death
Robert Maxwell met with Jules Kroll from
his penthouse hotel suite at the Helmsley
Palace Hotel in mid-October 1991. The
coincidences between Maxwell and Jeffrey
Epstein are too startling to overlook. The
location of the Helmsley Palace in the days
before Leona Helmsley was hauled off to jail

for tax evasion is where Epstein kept his offices.

Kroll owned a private investigation firm specializing in helping politicians, corporate CEOs and the uber wealthy. He also helped pioneer an industry whose mission it was to keep scandals out of the papers. This would be carefully crafted as "mitigating risk".

With the recent death of John Towers who along with his daughter perished when their commuter plane fell out of the sky crashing and bursting into flames, Maxwell was uneasy. The 50-year-old Kroll wore his trademark suspenders and held an oversized cigar. He and Maxwell both did business with Russia and by now he was known in the press as an international gumshoe. Kroll however prided himself on being more than this. Governments hired him to find stolen money and other assets spirited out of countries.

He and his two investigators followed the massively overweight Maxwell to the patio. He was concerned the room was wired before his arrival.

Maxwell who was not known to show fear looked Kroll in the eye. "There are people out to get me," he began. "To destroy my empire, my life and my business." The three men were accustomed to the well-placed paranoia of high-powered businessmen and nodded sympathetically.

"They want to destroy my life in any way they can and cripple me financially." Gesturing dramatically with his hands he pointed to Kroll, "I want you to find out who is behind this plot."

Kroll plucked the cigar out of his mouth. "Put together a list of suspicious and unexplained events," he instructed.

At the end of the meeting the men bade their goodbyes. Before Maxwell could complete his task he was dead and Kroll was never formally hired.

Robert Maxwell's shady dealings were not new. He had been shuffling around assets and exaggerating his net worth for over 40 years. Still underleveraged but with unbounded bravado in early March of 1991 Maxwell purchased the *New York Daily News*.

One thing happened during Maxwell's stay in New York which this author believes is the reason Ghislaine made the United States, and in particular New York, her home after her father's demise.

Robert Pirie, Maxwell's investment banker and the president of Rothschild, Inc., recalled what happened the day after his purchase of the New York newspaper. "I picked him up at his boat. He liked Chinese food, so I decided to take him to Fu's, which is the best Chinese restaurant in the city. As we drove up First Avenue, people would recognize him, and open their car doors and come out and shake his hand. At Fu's, the entire restaurant got up on its feet and started clapping. He was so overwhelmed. He told me, 'In my whole life in London, no one's ever acted like this. I'm here a month and look what's happening.'"

His widow, Betty, would echo the sentiment when she told people he had immigrated to the wrong country explaining that no one in Britain understood a character like him and that everything would have "come his way" had he lived in America.

Americans also liked his wit as a story teller. John Campi, Vice President of promotions for the *Daily News* recounted an anecdote Maxwell shared with him about Leonid Breshnev, the General Secretary of the Communist Party of the Soviet Union. Maxwell told him that Breshnev asked him what would have happened if Khrushchev had been assassinated instead of John F. Kennedy to which he replied, "Well, one thing is for sure. Mr. Onassis would not have married Mrs. Khrushchev."

Seymour Hersh

Seymour M. Hersh is a well-respected investigative journalist who in 1970 won a Pulitzer Prize for his work exposing the My Lai Massacre and its cover-up during the Vietnam War. He also wrote an article in 1975 published in *The New York Times* titled *Family Plans to Sue CIA Over Suicide in Drug Test*. It discussed the suicide of Frank Olson who committed suicide in 1953 after being made an unwilling participant in a Central Intelligence Agency drug experiment and that the family planned to sue the agency over his "wrongful death". Subsequent to the publication of his article Frank Olson's widow and three children were invited by President Gerald Ford to the White House where they received an apology.

In his book, *The Samson Option: Israel's Nuclear Arsenal and American Foreign Policy* published in 1991 he exposed Robert Maxwell and his foreign editor, Nicholas Davies as being spies for Mossad. Hersh included intimate details on how Davies tipped off the Israeli embassy about the whereabouts of nuclear technician and peace activist Mordechai Vanunu's whereabouts – which led to his being kidnapped by Mossad and imprisoned in Israel.

Mordechai Vanunu

In the summer of 1976 Vanunu responded to an ad as a trainee technician to work at Israel's nuclear plant in Dimona. Once accepted he was sent to take courses in physics, chemistry, math and English. He passed all the exams and began working at a secret underground weapons facility at the Dimona nuclear plant in the Negev desert in southern Israel. When they began to use Lithium Six – which is a deadly chemical agent used for hydrogen bombs – Vanunu, a pacifist, became alarmed.

The job lasted through November 1985. His security file contains the notation that he had displayed "left-wing and pro-Arab beliefs".

"I was terrified at what Israel was capable of and felt that I had to prevent a nuclear holocaust in the Middle East. I took 60 pictures of the processing plant then I left Israel in 1986 and went to Australia," he says.

Vanunu renounced his Jewish faith becoming a Christian. He lived in a hostel and supported himself by working as a hotel dishwasher and as a taxi driver. He was adamantly against war, and read books on philosophy and politics.

While in Australia he met Oscar Guerrero, a freelance journalist. Vanunu felt an ethical obligation to tell the world he felt Israel posed a threat with its nuclear capability. Guerrero agreed to write this extraordinary story and contacted the British *Sunday Time's* office in Madrid. To investigate properly *The Sunday Times* sent one of their journalist's, Peter Hounam, to Sydney, Australia to interview Vanunu and look over his documents. In violation of his non-disclosure agreement Vanunu revealed his knowledge of the Israeli nuclear secrets and showed him the photographs he had secretly taken. Hounam, assured that what Vanunu was saying was legit, asked him to accompany him to London to meet personally with the editor-in-chief.

Guerrero, feeling that Hounam was cheating him out of his exclusive story chased after Vanunu and met up with him in London. Both men, frustrated by the delay of *The Sunday Times*, decided to contact Robert Maxwell's *Sunday Mirror* and offered them the story. It was a disastrous step as they spoke with Nicholas Davies who told Maxwell and then immediately tipped off the Mossad revealing Vanunu's whereabouts.

The Mossad had a problem and were not sure how to handle it. They had a couple of options. They could discredit Vanunu in the media or send assassins and have him murdered. Either option disposed of their problem. However, when they saw the photographs, they realized they would not be able to readily discredit him because if they were published every nuclear physicist would recognize the equipment as legitimately being part of their nuclear arsenal.

They decided to interrogate him instead and find out how he had gone about gathering such photographs. Until the Mossad's kidnappers arrived in London, they contacted Robert Maxwell with instructions. He was to publish a large photograph of Vanunu with an accompanying story about Oscar Guerrero being a "liar and a cheat" and that Vanunu's claim about Israel's nuclear capability was a "hoax".

Instead of picking Vanunu up from the streets of London they decided on having one of their female operatives seduce him and lure him to a more remote location where they could abduct him in a less conspicuous manner.

Cheryl Bentov is an American real estate agent and a former Israeli Mossad spy who in 1986 used the alias "Cindy" to persuade Mordechai Vanunu to go with "her sister's apartment in Rome". When they arrived at the location, Vanunu was overpowered by three men and injected with a paralyzing drug. An ambulance arrived and Vanunu's limp body was removed out of the building on a stretcher. Bystanders did not suspect the medics were in fact spies and in the process of kidnapping him.

Within three days he was back in Israel where he was charged with treason and espionage and placed in prison for 18 years – 11 of these were spent in solitary confinement. After his release in 2004 he was subjected to severe restrictions on what he can publicly say and where he can go. To present day, Mordechai Vanunu remains a prisoner of Israel and endures constant harassment by the Mossad.

Spy Allegations

Seymour Hersh also included in his book that Nicholas Davies was involved in Israeli arms sales and that his boss, Robert Maxwell, was also connected to the Mossad.

Davies's former wife, Janet Fielding, confirmed all to Hersh. Davies had just left his wife for Robert Maxwell's secretary, Andrea Martin. Fielding, then a 33-year-old actress told London newspapers that she gave Seymour Hersh two documents she found in their home when she went to collect her belongings during their bitter split. The letters appeared to be from U.S. arms dealers to Davies indicating he was involved in weapons deals.

Robert Maxwell and Nicholas Davies immediately declared the allegations "a complete and a total lie, ludicrous and a total invention". On October 23, 1991 they filed a libel suit against the book's publisher, Faber & Faber Ltd and two days later filed another one against Hersh.

Seymour Hersh stood his ground, "What I have written is true and I stand by it," he said at a news conference. "I am prepared to defend it in any place I have to." His book also reports that Israeli Prime Minister Yitzhak Shamir has passed top-secret American intelligence, stolen by convicted spy Jonathan Pollard to the Soviet Union.

One of Hersh's major sources for the book was former intelligence agent Ari Ben-Menashe who claimed he'd worked closely with Davies and who made the charges to Congress about the Iran-Contra affair.

Ari Ben-Menashe

Ari Ben-Menashe was an arms dealer for the Mossad. During the 1980s he was a top intelligence officer for Israel and assigned to a special unit of Israeli military intelligence. He was born in Iran and emigrated to Israel as a teenager.

He traveled the world on behalf of the Mossad brokering Israeli-sponsored arms sales to Iran during the war with Iraq in the 1980s. In 1989 he was arrested in the United States on charges of selling military aircraft to Iran.

He was put into a small jail cell in Manhattan – in the same correction facility that Jeffrey Epstein would one day find himself and where on August 10, 2019 he would be found dead. Epstein's death was labeled a suicide.

Ben-Menashe was not accustomed to being in jail, nor to the squalid conditions of the jail. He said, "The place was more like a third-class, flea-bag hotel."

The guards informed him that previous occupants included John Gotti, the Mafia godfather and Joe Doherty, the Irish revolutionary.

Frustrated and upset that at the age of 37 he hadn't been allowed to post bail because the federal prosecutor considered him a flight risk and indignant at the whole episode because he had once walked through the corridors of Ronald Reagan's White House as a welcome visitor, he vowed to find a way out.

He was not happy with the idea proposed to him by the two attorneys that Israel assigned to him. They proposed he plead guilty, serve his sentence and afterwards Israel would find him an obscure place in the world so he could live out the remainder of his days. He refused.

Instead he came up with a plan to get himself release. He would claim he was a writer working undercover of assignment. To pull this off he would need from Nicholas Davis an affidavit claiming he was working on a book and from Robert Maxwell a statement that the book was already under contract.

He had proposed that Davis ghostwrite the book for him and that Maxwell publish it under his Macmillan publishing house in New York. However, he pushed too hard because he also told them he wanted to be paid $750,000.00 as a "down payment". They passed on his offer. And what this did was to induce a state of anger of such proportions that he knew one day he would extract his revenge.

Helping Seymour Hersh with the information he needed to write *The Samson Option* partly quenched his thirst for payback.

What should be noted is that during 1990 when Ben-Menashe was revealing all the dirt on Robert Maxwell and Nicholas Davies at no point did he mention Jeffrey Epstein as being involved with Ghislaine Maxwell.

After Epstein's arrest, however, he has been on several shows alleging he "knew" Epstein and that Epstein was Ghislaine's "boyfriend" and was given Robert Maxwell's blessing for their "little" extortion trafficking scheme.

This is not true.

Further, Martin Dillon, who is one of the authors of *Robert Maxwell, Israel's Superspy* researched Robert Maxwell's life very carefully for their book. Dillon is emphatic they found no evidence of Jeffrey Epstein as being in Robert Maxwell or Ghislaine's life during while he was alive.

The Maxwells, it should be noted, were fond of taking photographs and videos. I was fortunate to have seen some of their personal videos with Ghislaine playing the part of hostess at Headington Hill Hall alongside her mother. Jeffrey Epstein wasn't in any of these videos either.

NINETEEN

The Death of Robert Maxwell

The last time Robert Maxwell was seen alive was onboard *The Lady Ghislaine* on November 5, 1991 at 4.25 a.m. He called a crew member asking that he turn up the air conditioning in his cabin. Twenty minutes later he called again and asked that it be

turned down. The crew remembers that
Maxwell seemed restless going in and out of
his cabin several times.

The trip began on October 31st at 6:30am in the
same manner that all his trips on *The Lady Ghislaine*
began. He flew on his private helicopter to Luton
airport, a small regional spot just outside of London,
where he boarded his private Gulfstream jet. Just before
11am he arrived in Gibraltar, where his yacht, was
waiting.

Maxwell had a nagging cold but he met with
various people while on his short getaway. On
November 4 the Lady Ghislaine docked at Santa Cruz in
Tenerife in the Canary Island and Maxwell decided to
go ashore. A cab was summoned to pick him up and the
driver, Arturo Hernandez Trujillo, was instructed by
Maxwell's Spanish speaking chef to take him to a good
restaurant.

The driver stopped at the San Andres restaurant
which Maxwell told him was not suitable. He asked him
to take him to a good hotel instead and was dropped off
at the Hotel Mencey. A five-star establishment on a
hillside in the residential part of the small port city.
Robert Maxwell ate his last meal there that evening.
Codfish cooked with clams and mushrooms. He ordered
three beers leaving the last one unfinished. Before going

back to the yacht he made another stop at Café Olimpo and had a coffee and a brandy. When he was done he used his walkie-talkie and called his crew alerting them he was on his way back. Three crew members and the captain, Angus Rankin, greeted him on his return at a little past 10pm that evening.

The yacht sailed from Santa Cruz, on the north end of Tenerife, around the Grand Canary Island to the east. It anchored about 200 yards from the beach near Los Cristianos at 9:30am.

No one suspected anything out of the ordinary had happened.

At 11:30am Captain Rankin called their Santa Cruz shipping agent Juan Hamilton exclaiming, "We cannot find the owner." He told him he sent people ashore, then added, "I think we've lost him overboard".

Wild stories began to circulate immediately. That he might have been urinating or vomiting over the rail and fell. And of mysterious unmarked vessels near the yacht.

Robert Maxwell's naked body was found arms splayed out, face staring into the sky, eyes wide open, enormous belly bobbing in the Atlantic Ocean by a fishing boat floating 19 to 20 miles from Gando on the other side of the neighboring island of Grand Canaria – more than 15 miles away from his 180-foot yacht.

Maxwell was missing for 14 hours before his body was finally recovered.

On 10:40pm on November 4th Robert Maxwell had a conversation with his son Ian from the Lady Ghislaine.

After exchanging business talk, they said their goodbyes.

"See you tomorrow," Ian said to his father.

"You bet," Maxwell replied.

He then spoke with his longtime attorney and confidant Samuel Pisar about an hour before he fell or was pushed of his yacht, *The Lady Ghislaine*.

By the time Maxwell's lifeless body was pulled out of the Atlantic Ocean Betty Maxwell and her daughter Ghislaine were already on a plane to the Canary Islands. John Jackson, a reporter for the *Mirror* flew with them and said of Betty, "There were no tears. She was quite composed."

He claims she said, "I'll tell you one thing. He would never kill himself. It's not suicide."

Robert Maxwell's body was airlifted to Las Palmas 20 miles away. Captain Jesus Fernandez Vaca was the person who first spotted the body from his helicopter. He told Jackson he believed Maxwell had been in the water for about 12 hours. Vaca added that when the body was pulled out no water came out of his lungs. "I have taken many, many bodies out of the sea and I can tell you for certain that he didn't drown."

According to Nicholas Davies, Maxwell had often talked to his personal assistant Andrea Martin about 'doing a Stonehouse' – disappearing like former Labor MP John Stonehouse, who in 1974, faked his death and travelled to Australia to start a new life.

Maxwell had apparently told Andrea, "I have thought it would be a wonderful way of ending one's life. Living in a lovely house with a swimming pool in the middle of nowhere and not a worry, not a thought for all the problems."

While an autopsy was being performed rumors about whether he fell or was pushed or died of a heart attack or some other occurrence became part of the conversation surrounding the death of Robert Maxwell. The rumors about his death continued for a very long time. In 1992 when *The Guardian* suggested Betty Maxwell had been part of a plot to fake his death, she filed a libel suit against them.

Betty tasked Ghislaine, who she thought of as the most practical and the one with the most experience in public speaking to give the reporters a speech the following day after their arrival. She spoke fluent Spanish and had gotten accustomed to public speaking with working with her father at the Oxford Club.

Wearing a red Maxwell tartan plaid suit Ghislaine spoke from the deck of the yacht. The night before she wore a blue Maxwell tartan plaid. This was no coincidence – it was in honor of her father who at some point must have boasted about having been a descendant of the famous Maxwell clan of Caerlaverock Castle. Although by the time of his death Ghislaine must have known the truth, she nonetheless proceeded as if the tall tale was true.

The moated triangular Caerlaverock castle was built in the 13th century in the southern coast of Scotland and was home to the Maxwell family until the 17th century. Ian Hoch changed his surname to Maxwell and pretended he was descendant from the Maxwell's of Caerlaverock. The Maxwell fake family history was so entrenched into the Hoch family that, not being able to differentiate fantasy from reality, Ghislaine Maxwell wore a suit made of 'Maxwell Tartan' on November 7, 1991 when she read a statement from *The Lady Ghislaine* thanking the Spanish authorities for their help in retrieving the body of her father.

She began by thanking the authorities in near perfect Castilian Spanish.

"On behalf of my mother and brothers," she began and went on to thank the police and military in Tenerife who had helped with the search for her father.

She then switched to English.

"I also want to take this opportunity to thank all the many hundreds of people who have sent messages of support to us at this very, very sad time.

"I want also to thank the press for their courtesy and consideration to my mother and to us at this time, which we appreciate very much."

She finished by saying: "Gracias a todos and thank you very much."

Ghislaine had her own feelings about how her father died. She believed he had been murdered. When she boarded the yacht her father had named after her in 1986 the night before she tore through her father's papers. John Jackson claimed, "Ghislaine rushed through the yacht's lounges and cabins, rifled drawers and cabinets, plucking documents indiscriminately and throwing them to the ground. She shouted to the crew, "I order you to shred immediately everything I have thrown on the floor."

Ghislaine "totally and utterly" denied the claims.

John added, "I didn't think anything of it at the time. We had no idea of his criminality. He was a great hero. Our newspaper described him as 'The man who saved the Mirror'."

An article written by *The Sydney Morning Herald* which appears to have been syndicated from *The Telegraph* reads:

"On November 5, 1991, the body of Maxwell's father, Robert, the plutocrat, British newspaper tycoon and – it would shortly transpire – arch embezzler, was found floating in the Atlantic Ocean off the coast of Tenerife, having fallen from his 55-metre luxury yacht, the Lady Ghislaine. The following day, his distraught daughter arrived in Tenerife by private jet. Boarding the yacht, which had been named in her honor, Ghislaine went to her father's quarters. Searching through his private papers, she found a reference to a New York financier who had been particularly helpful to him in squirrelling away misbegotten funds offshore. Shortly afterwards, Ghislaine flew to New York, to escape the shame of her father and make a new life for herself. One of the first people she reached out to was that financier. His name was Jeffrey Epstein."

≈

During the trial of Ghislaine Maxwell in late 2021 it was revealed, via one of Jeffrey Epstein's pilots, David Rodgers, that she was one of the passengers on the second flight of Epstein's newly acquired Hawker Siddely 125 on July 26, 1991. Ghislaine knew Epstein at least four months before her father died—but not before this. In her own deposition, which I cite in this book, she states she met him in 1991.

~

Tom Bower, who has written several books on Robert Maxwell and has known Ghislaine since she was 11 wrote that she had been given an envelope with £15,000 to give to the captain of the yacht but that she was so "appalled at the state of the yacht and the way the crew denigrated her father's reputation that she refused to hand over the cash."

~

During the time his body was examined for the autopsy Betty Maxwell was guided by the family's long trusted advisor and attorney, Samuel Pisar. Although Pisar was based in Paris he was an Auschwitz survivor and had become very close to her husband – perhaps his only confidant and provided him with sage business advise. It was Pisar who helped pave the way for Maxwell into Israel's business community. Neeman has an impressive resume

He consoled Betty and told her the most important thing was to arrange for his body to be transferred to Israel. To that end he told her he would instruct Julio Claverie, the Canary Islands attorney the family had retained to handle the Spanish end, while he would get, Ya'atov Neeman, in Jerusalem who was another of Maxwell's attorneys to handle the funeral arrangements.

Neeman has an impressive resume that most people fail to recognize when writing about Robert Maxwell.

Born in Tel Aviv in 1939 – meaning born in Palestine – he went on to study law at New York University after serving in the army. Upon his return to Israel he founded the law firm Herzog, Fox & Ne'eman with the future President of Israel Chaim Herzog.

Ghislaine, who stayed with her mother, fended off press inquiries surrounding her statement that she believed her father had been murdered. Neither she or her mother knew, at this point, the extent of the financial crisis that was ever-present in the mind of Robert Maxwell just before his death. Whether Kevin or Ian made any mention of it to their mother or the rest of the family no one knows. However, it must have been a burden for them both because they were the intermediaries who acted on behalf of their father.

On Friday, November 8, 1991 just before 3am the Maxwell family boarded the plane that would carry Robert Maxwell's body to Israel. As dawn broke and the plane entered Israeli airspace two Israeli fighter planes appeared on either side.

"We are your official escort," a crackled voice said echoing into the pilots' headphones.

Waiting to greet Ghislaine, Philip and her mother was Ya'atov Neeman and some of the senior airport officials. Neeman accompanied them and helped them check into the King David Hotel in Jerusalem where they were given the presidential suite. Meanwhile the rest of the Maxwell family along with their spouses began to arrive in one limousine after another.

Ghislaine and her sisters huddled together to talk about what each would wear to the funeral and used the phones to make appointments to get their hair done.

The following morning Ya'ztov Neeman arrived at Betty's door. He had good news, he told her. "It is going to be a state funeral. Yitzhak Shamir has ordered it. Bob will lie in the Hall of Nations."

A state funeral was only held for presidents and prime ministers. Robert Maxwell was the exception to this rule.

And after she thanked him and him to thank the Prime Minister he replied, "You can tell him yourself. They will all be there."

On a mild Monday morning on the 11th of November President Chaim Herzog intoned over the body of Robert Maxwell as it lay in Israel's Hall of the Nation. His words filled the room packed with dignitaries, "He scaled the heights. Kings and barons besieged his doorstep. He was a figure of almost mythological stature. An actor on the world stage, bestriding the globe, as Shakespeare says, like a colossus."

The Kaddish, the prayer usually said by the closest male relative, was recited by Samuel Pisar.

Philip broke down in tears as he spoke. He said, "We salute you. We love you. We need you. We miss you. We cry for your presence. Whether by land, sea or air, you can travel no more and our hearts can bear no more pain. May you rest in peace." His brother Ian embraced him immediately afterwards in an effort to console him.

Among those who attended the prestigious funeral were six serving and former heads of the Mossad as well as former and present Prime Ministers including Yitzak Shamir, Ariel Sharon and Shimon Peres. Also in attendance was Soviet émigré Natan Sharansky, a large number of Ukrainian children whom Maxwell helped emigrate from Chernobyl after the nuclear disaster, his bankers from Nikko Securities in London. Hundreds of Israelis also paid tribute and were in attendance.

After the solemn tribute the Maxwells climbed into their limousines and were driven to the cemetery. Robert Maxwell's nude body covered only with a 'tallit' – a fringed prayer shawl and without the casket laid on a stretcher near the open pit that was to be his grave.

Around the perimeter of the cemetery were police keeping dozens of journalists from intruding into the sacred ceremony.

Former Prime Minister Shimon Peres stepped forward as the Maxwell family stood side by side with pride fighting back tears as they said their final farewell to the man who had ruled their lives. He said, "He is closing the circle of life that knew want and plenty, danger and grandeur, but never surrender and despair." Then he paused and fixed his eyes on Betty. In a loud firm voice he added, "He has done more for Israel than can today be told."

As the sun began to drop behind the Mount of Olives the gravediggers lowered Maxwell's body deep into the hollow grave. Four of the mourners held the tallith over the opening so that no one could see what was happening below. As is customary in Israel, slabs of stone were lowered into the pit covering his naked body. The men then solemnly handed the family their shovels. One by one each one scooped up fresh dirt throwing it into the open grave where it landed over the slabs. The shovels were passed on and everyone who attended joined in the ceremony.

A little over one hour later the grief-stricken family bade their farewell to the solemn looking dignitaries and piled into the baggage-laden limousines. They were driven by armed men back to the airport where their chartered airplane awaited. The was no *shiva* – the traditional week-long mourning period immediately following the burial where the closest family members discuss their loss and comfort one another. Instead, the Maxwells went back to their homes where they would begin to pick up the pieces of their shattered lives and re-invent themselves.

They returned to a media frenzy. Betty Maxwell was said to have "grown numb" to the public's battering. Ghislaine who had become fond of telling people who asked her about the origins of her French first name, "I've been told it means ray of sunshine," and of basking in the limelight began walking around in a blonde wig in order to avoid being recognized. She was said by all to be the one most like her father. By the time he was 21 he had reinvented himself several times over. If he did it, so could she. It was this conviction that kept her steady where others would have collapsed.

Also feeling the heat were the bankers facing legal and regulatory scrutiny. Dan Brockbank, a spokesman for the National Bank of Westminster said, "Any banking relationship can be seen as a four-legged stool, involving the honesty and integrity of both the bank and the client. We could not know that in Mr. Maxwell's case, two of the legs were missing."

Peter Jay, a former British Ambassador to Washington who worked as Maxwell's chief of staff from 1986 to 1989 said, "He was a peasant to the roots of his fingernails, with his peasant's mistrust of others.

Things were run on a need-to-know principle: if you needed to know, you weren't told".

No one it appeared saw the warning signs despite the fact that they had been there from the very start. As early as 1969 Maxwell had shown his colors when Leasco, an American company owned by Saul Steinberg, agreed to acquire Pergamon in June 1969. Steinberg discovered he had been misled by Maxwell, then a Member of Parliament, about the true value of Pergamon. This was followed by the British government declaring Maxwell unfit to run a public company in 1971. It was discovered that he had used transactions with his private companies to inflate the profits of Pergamon. The deal with Leasco fell apart and twenty years later bankers moaned that the trust they placed in Robert Maxwell had been abused.

Even in Israel people felt the reverberations of his fall. All the Prime Ministers, past and present, pretended as if nothing had happened. Those who put signs "Maxwell Buy Me" in their cars yanked them off feeling as if they too had been duped.

Kevin Maxwell, 33, was charged on two counts of conspiracy and six of theft totaling more than $233 million. Ian Maxwell, 36, was charged with one count of conspiracy. Their American advisor, Larry Trachtenberg, 39, was also charged with fraud and theft. The three men were arrested following a seven-month investigation into the disappearance of millions of dollars of pension funds. The three face a total of 15 charges of conspiracy and theft, many of them relating to the period after Maxwell's mysterious death.

Kevin Maxwell told the press, "After seven months of trial by rumor, of trial by innuendo, of trial by selective press leaks, and of prejudicial media reporting, I am really looking forward to being able to defend myself in a court of law where I intend to vigorously and strenuously contest all and any charges against me."

In 1996 the £12 million trial acquitted the three men but the court record states, "Nonetheless, conduct can be blameworthy without being criminal." Newspaper accounts wrote about how Kevin Maxwell knew about the substantial plundering of pension funds for the benefit of Maxwell Communication Corporation and of his father's practice of obtaining unsecured cash loans. He knew this had not been disclosed in reports to trustees but he did not take steps to bring the matter to their attention. Further, that he was aware "disclosures to bankers, regulators and others lacked frankness". That when he was interviewed by inexperienced investigators from the pension watchdog that he presented everything in a favorable light.

The report makes it clear Kevin did his father's bidding as the debts piled up and knew towards the end of

1990 there were tremendous strains on the finances of the private companies which were borrowing on substantial scale from the pension funds. Every morning father and son would have a meeting or a conversation at which point Maxwell senior would give instructions as to the manner of payments to banks or cooperating companies. Kevin explained that his he had "a combative relationship with his father and they had rows". He explained that his father would always tell him it was his money and he would make the decision.

Ian was found to have a less prominent role but that he signed many of the documents without considering their implications and that he failed in his duties as a director of Bishopsgate Investment Management—which controlled some of the pension funds.

Larry Trachtenberg, a close friend of Kevin's, was found to "have little experience in business". However, he played a significant role in the arrangement for the use of the shares from the pension funds. Trachtenberg received a salary of £200,000 per year as an executive of Bishopsgate. It was discovered he knowingly signed a letter about one transaction he knew was untrue. In 1990 he also received a bonus of £250,000. After the dust settled Trachtenberg went to work for Kevin Maxwell at Telemonde.

Robert Maxwell, the report concluded, operated a policy of "divide and rule" even with his sons, refusing to allow them to work together.

The auditors of Maxwell Communications Corporation, Coopers & Lybrand who became part of PricewaterhouseCoopers were criticized for their role which earned them £1.48 million in fees. They knew that many of Robert Maxwell's transactions included his regular use of pension fund money to support the group as well as supplying the minimum disclosure of financial information.

Coopers was found to bear a major responsibility for failing to report to the trustees of the pension scheme Maxwell's numerous abuses and that the company failed in their duties as independent auditors. They were fined £3.4 million for failing to blow the whistle on the financial irregularities they witnessed. Their employees Stephen Wootten, Nicholas Parker, Ian Steere and John Cowling—all of whom were responsible for Maxwell's accounts—were ordered to pay £111.050 fines.

The senior account Peter Walsh died before the matter was resolved. He was heavily criticized by having noted that all was "good" during the time Maxwell's use of pension money was not identified in the accounts.

Eric Sheinberg of Goldman Sachs, the U.S. investment bank that acted as Robert Maxwell's broker on a number of transactions were heavily criticized. Sheinberg was regarded as a "god-like" figure in the Mirror Group Newspapers (MGM) boardroom. He earned huge profits for his bank from the "manipulation of the market in Maxwell shares".

The inspectors stated: "Goldman Sachs were the investment bank with whom Robert Maxwell principally dealt when purchasing MCC and MGB shares and bear a substantial responsibility in respect of the manipulation that occurred in the market."

In the end no one was held responsible for the criminal liability of what was at the time Britain's biggest and most dramatic post-war financial scandal. Everyone knew a massive fraud had taken place. There were hundreds of lawyers, bankers, accountants and investigators who poured over the financial documents. Those affected by it were flabbergasted. It appeared to all as if there was one law for the rich and another for the poor.

It was several months after the death of Robert Maxwell that Betty discovered her husband's internal organs, examined after the autopsy, were still in Spain. Later, the family would learn his brain had been left behind sitting in a jar.

The last conversation Ghislaine Maxwell had with her father was in his office before he took off for his ill-fated trip. In an interview with *Vanity Fair* she shared their last words. "He was looking for an apartment in New York—a sort of pied-à-terre, where he could talk and have meetings—and he wanted me to help him. He asked me to go see a particular apartment. He said, 'If you like it, I'll make time to see it and come to New York.'"

For the next several weeks Ghislaine reeled at the headlines. Her beloved father had fallen off his pedestal and was called a battery of offending words: a rogue, crook, bully, thief, megalomaniac, gangster, a former employee claimed he had her call him Mr. Maxwell in bed and that he had a thing for orgies with midget Filipino hookers. Other women with whom he'd slept throughout the years crawled out of every crevice to tell their tales about how Robert Maxwell wasn't a good lover but had been generous.

Ghislaine was also stunned to hear her father had proposed marriage to Andrea Martin who had begun working for him at the age of 18 in 1982 and who as recent as July 1990 had flown with him to Berlin on a business trip. She'd known about the gifts her father lavished on the good-looking blonde: the shiny new BMW he gave her on her birthday, the use of his personal American Express card, and how he coddled her.

Even her brother, Kevin, knew that it was important to keep on Andrea's good side." Declining his proposal she ran off with the editor of the *Mirror* Nick Davies with whom she was having an affair. There was not a moment without having some disturbing tale or event disrupting her life and the lives of her family.

Betty Maxwell told *Vanity Fair*, "My daughter Ghislaine has no money, no trusts, no funds anywhere." She added, "Neither of my children had any money. Their father never gave them any money."

Fact is the family's assets were frozen. Kevin's house was put up for sale as were the 'Lady Ghislaine' yacht and the Gulfstream Jet. Their passports were also seized.

A friend who knew Ghislaine during this period said, "She was catatonic."

She had been living in a large comfortable apartment her father arranged the company to provide to her in addition to the £100,000 he paid her as a salary and was forced to vacate it. She moved into a small apartment that was literally void of furnishings.

Ghislaine moaned to a friend, "They took everything—everything—even the cutlery."

In an interview Ghislaine gave to Vanity Press she said of her late father, "He wasn't a crook. A thief to me is somebody who steals money. Did he put it in his own pocket? Did he run off with the money? No. And that's my definition of a crook."

"I'm surviving—just," she said. "But I can't just die quietly in a comer. I have to believe that something good will come out of this mess. It's sad for my mother. It's sad to have lost my dad. It's sad for my brothers. But I would say we'll be back. Watch this space."

～

The lawsuit commenced by Robert Maxwell and Nicholas Davies against author Seymour Hersh where he alleged they were both spies slowly disappeared. Davies whose ex-wife produced two documents supporting the claims – one of them linking to an arms deal in Ohio – did not pursue the case. And with Robert Maxwell dead, it was left to his estate and attorneys to handle the matter. In August 1994 an out of court settlement was reached. By accepting the settlement whose terms were confidential Seymour Hersh ended the libel suit he initiated against Maxwell and the *Mirror Group*.

One of the lawyers for the *Mirror Group* made a public statement, "Mr. Hersh is an author of excellent reputation and of the highest integrity who would never write anything which he did not believe to be true and that he was in this instance fully justified in writing what he did."

The Mirror Group apologized to Hersh and to his publishers Faber & Faber agreeing to pay them damages and as well as their legal obligations.

~

In a 2003 article written by Alan D. Abbey for the *Jerusalem Post*, now scrubbed, Isabel Maxwell, one of Ghislaine's older sisters said, "My father was certainly a patriot and helped in back business and political channels between governments. But that did not and does not make him a spy. It's just that it's so much sexier to call him that and it sells more copy."

She bristles when anyone refers to him as a spy and prefers he be "remembered for his accomplishments, chief among them the spreading of scientific knowledge through his publishing company, Pergamon Press as well as by grants and loans to scientists around the world."

TWENTY

Jeffrey Epstein

———————

The Plaza Hotel in New York City is an architectural delight and one of the city's prized historical landmarks. Its design echoes a French chateau and when built only the finest materials from across the world were used. Throughout its majestic entrance and in its public spaces there are 1,650 over-sized chandeliers. The hotel took two years to complete at a cost of $12.5 million and debuted on October 1, 1907.

Alfred Vanderbilt, the great-grandson of Cornelius Vanderbilt, and the wealthiest man in the world at the time, made headlines when he arrived in an ornate horse-drawn carriage at the entrance and stepped out – becoming the first guest to book a room.

Prior to Robert Maxwell's death two Jewish organizations planned to honor him with awards. Celebrations of this sort are usually for the benefit of the organization granting the award and so they invited Betty to accept them on his behalf.

In her book, *A Life of My Own*, she writes:

"I was subsequently approached by two Jewish organizations that had made plans to confer awards on Bob prior to his death and wanted me to receive them in his stead. One was the Zionist Organization of America. The other was the YIVO Institute for Jewish research which wanted to pay tribute to Bob's commitment to Jewish history and culture. I left for New York towards the end of November and was away for three days."

The YIVO Institute placed a notice in the Social Events section of *The New York Times* through which they sold additional tickets to the black-tie affair scheduled for November 24, 1991.

In the Oak Room, under its vaulted ceiling and elegantly paneled walls, Robert Maxwell's widow, Betty with her daughter Ghislaine sat in the honoree's table. Tony Randall, best known for his role as Felix Unger in *The Odd Couple* has accepted the role of presenting the award and sits with the Maxwells. Occupying the seat between Ghislaine and her mother sits Jeffrey Epstein.

Betty took the very first photo showing Ghislaine and Epstein together. Almost two weeks after burying her father in Israel Ghislaine is smiling coyly at him and he grins back.

Jeffrey Epstein, who 20 years earlier drove a New York City cab, had become accustomed to asking women questions of a sexual nature. His Brooklyn accent didn't make these unexpected dagger-like comments sound appealing. Although some women succumbed to his boorish advances because of the way he flashed his wealth. Ghislaine Maxwell, who inherited her father's crude manner, thought him witty and charming. While there is no way of knowing what they were talking about at moment the photo was taken, we do know that Tony Randall appears somewhat taken aback by what he has overheard.

Jeffrey Epstein has not honored the dress code. He did not arrive in black tie. The man who is most comfortable in a pair of jeans and $500 slippers with the words 'Screw U' on them is wearing white tie. White tie is reserved for very formal events like evening weddings for the very rich or state dinners or evening.

Donald Trump, who Ghislaine counts among her friends, purchased the hotel in 1988. While I was not able to confirm whether Trump was a guest, it is fair to say he may have stopped by to pay his respects to Betty and Ghislaine Maxwell.

During Ghislaine Maxwell's deposition in the slander lawsuit with Virginia Giuffre she was questioned about how and when she met Jeffrey Epstein.

Q. When did you first meet Jeffrey?

A. At some point in 1991.

Q. How were you introduced to Jeffrey?

A. Some friend introduced us.

Q. Can you describe your relationship back in 1991, was it friendship or was it girlfriend relationship or was it a work relationship, what was your relationship in 1991?

A. It was just friendly.

The tribute at The Plaza is a full circle moment for Robert Maxwell as this is one of the places where J. Edgar Hoover, Director of the FBI had his room wired in the 1950s.

Ironically, it is also the hotel where Hoover himself was seen at a boy's sex party in 1959 by Susan Rosentiel, the fourth wife of mobster and bootlegger Lewis Rosentiel.

In Anthony Summers book, *Official and Confidential: The Secret Life of J. Edgar Hoover* he writes that Susan "recalled seeing Hoover with a red dress on and a black feather boa around his neck.....After about half an hour, some boys came, like before. This time they're dressed in leather. And Hoover has a Bible. He wanted one of the boys to read from the Bible, and he read, I forget which passage." She then said the other boy engaged "in sexual activity with Hoover".

Lewis Rosentiel, it should be noted, was Roy Cohn's mentor, who in 1973 became the attorney and mentor to Donald Trump when he and his father, Fred were accused by the government of violating the Fair Housing Act by refusing to rent apartments at the Trumps' Shore Haven properties in Brooklyn to black and Latino applicants.

It is alleged that Cohn and Rosentiel ran a child blackmail ring they used to blackmail government officials in order to keep them from going after the mob. Cohn and Trump were joined at the hip until Cohn's body was ravaged by AIDS, at which point Trump, simply stopped seeing him. Cohn died of AIDS-related complications on August 2, 1986.

By the time of the YIVO event honoring the life of Robert Maxwell at The Plaza Hotel newspapers everywhere were ablaze with the news of Maxwell's enormous theft and crimes that left his family bankrupt and his sons, Kevin and Ian, facing criminal prosecution.

The details included that Robert Maxwell had committed massive fraud by plundering his employees' pension funds, had stolen monies from two of his public companies, had moved large sums of money in and out of secret family trusts in Leichtenstein, had illegally propped up the share price of Maxwell Communications Corporation, and had incurred debts of more than $5 billion.

Before his death Maxwell confided in his Russian mistress Kira Vladina, "My family won't inherit anything when I die. The only ones who deserve anything are my youngest, Ghislaine and Kevin. I adore both of them. Kevin is so much like me and Ghislaine is a friend."

≈

Five months after the arrest of her brothers Kevin and Ian on fraud and theft charges, Ghislaine Maxwell was seen in November of 1992 boarding the Concorde on a flight from London to New York.

An article published by The *Mail on Sunday* written by Michael Robotham and dated November 15, 1992 reads:

"In public relations terms, it was an unmitigated disaster. Ghislaine Maxwell, the youngest and most pulchritudinous of the disgraced tycoon's children, was photographed boarding Concorde to return to her adopted city, New York.

The bankers cheated by her father and pensioners left destitute as a result of Robert Maxwell's wickedness were incandescent with anger.

A one-way trip on Concorde costs more than £2,000 – an awful lot of money for a young woman reported to be living on a 'meagre' £80,000 trust fund set up by her father.

But her departure for New York is notable for a very different reason. Unnoticed by almost everybody, travelling with her was a greying, plumpish, middle-aged American businessman who managed to avoid the photographers.

It is to this man that 30-year-old Ghislaine has turned to ease the heartache of her father's shame.

His name is Jeffrey Epstein, a shadowy, almost maverick New York 'property developer' who, for over a year, has helped Ghislaine become a coveted fixture on the Manhattan social scene. During the last year, say friends, she has fallen in love with him, and the couple are inseparable."

Stuart Pivar, an art collector and controversial scientist, is an old friend of Epstein's. Pivar in a *Mother Jones* interview claims "Epstein brought Maxwell to New York in 1991 after her father died" and put him "in charge of Ghislaine while she was profoundly depressed from the death of her father".

Stuart Pivar, who was a friend of Andy Warhol, gave a revealing interview in a *Mother Jones* article about Epstein who he said had been his "best friend for decades".

"Jeffrey-how to put this? Jeffrey came into the concept of thought and science and all with no knowledge whatsoever about anything. He really didn't know a goddamn thing. I don't even believe that he taught math. Oh, Jeffrey once told me that he studied math with the Unabomber."

The *Unabomber* was a man named Ted Kaczynski who is an American terrorist and former mathematics teacher. He is said to have been a mathematics prodigy and an experiment of the Central Intelligence Agency's Project MK-Ultra, the CIA's research into mind control.

Stuart Pivar on how he met Epstein:

"One day in the early 1970s a friend of mine brought me to Jimmy Goldsmith's mansion on the east side. And I walked in, and there in the grandiose lobby was a grand piano, and there was someone playing with great virtuosity. And it was Jeffrey Epstein. That's how I met him."

Sir James "Jimmy" Goldsmith was an MI6 spy. He is described in a now scrubbed *New York Times* article as "a member of the British Secret Intelligence Services" and the private financier who handles "Israel's account" for Conrad Black's Hollinger International.

If Pivar's recollection is correct it suggests that Epstein knew him during his teaching days at Dalton—and maybe even before depending on how early Pivar interprets the early '70s.

Jeffrey Epstein allegedly worked under Jimmy Hollinger's tutelage.

Hollinger International is connected to all the players we see in Epstein's later years. Leslie Wexner, Canada's Bronfman family, and Henry Kissinger were on the company's advisory board.

In Epstein's black book is the name and contact info Goldsmith's daughter Jemimah. She is his eldest of three children he had with Annabel—the socialite known for the celebrated nightclub. Jemimah was also the one with whom he had the strongest attachment. Sir

James Goldsmith was a distant cousin and longtime business associate of the Rothschilds.

TWENTY-ONE

Jeffrey Epstein, Brooklyn Born

———————

Jeffrey Epstein and Ghislaine Maxwell could not have been more different or more alike.

He was born to Seymour G. Epstein (1916-1991) and Paula (nee Stolofsky, 1918-2004). Seymour's parents had emigrated from Russia and settled into the

Brooklyn neighborhood of New York City. Paula's parents arrived in the United States as Lithuanian refugees.

Seymour toiled as a laborer for the New York City Parks Department. His mother was a stay-at-home mom until Jeffrey and his brother, Mark, were in high school, at which point she went to work at a local school. They were, by all appearances, a normal middle-class family. The family was able to afford piano lessons for their two boys and in 1967 Epstein at the age of 14 attended Interlochen National Music summer camp in Michigan.

Beverly Donatelli was Epstein's neighbor and two years older than he. She recalled that as a kid he was "Chubby with curly hair and a 'hee-hee' laugh. Because he had a flair for math he skipped two grades in school and so they graduated at the same time.

Gary Grossberg was a friend—one year younger than Epstein who remembers him fondly. "He was a diamond in the rough, you see. People recognized Jeffrey's brilliance very early on. But he had a gift for recognizing opportunities very quickly.

Jeffrey Epstein attended Lafayette High School. James Rosen, a former classmate said, "Lafayette was a city school. It was functional. There was nothing special about it."

Early on the neighborhood of Sea Gate was 90 percent Italian. There was some anti-Semitism. Blacks had begun to move in. The Italians didn't want the Jews or the Blacks there. As with many city schools there was a lot of fighting.

Jeffrey Epstein practiced piano while his friends were on the beach and he worked on his prized stamp collection.

By the time he is 16-years-old he is taking advanced math classes at Cooper Union. Because of a generous endowment the school is free. This isn't an Ivy League school and there are many other students who *tawk* with a Brooklyn accent. He doesn't stand out but neither does he stick around long enough to graduate. He still lives with his parents and then decides to take courses at New York University. When he was deposed for one of numerous lawsuits, he was asked how long he had attended college. He responded, "Two years".

In the summer, Jeffrey drove taxi-cabs for spending money. He is also said to have been a roofer. Fixing the roof in other people's houses. In all, there was nothing extraordinary about him other than his aptitude for numbers. One day he dropped out of New York University and landed himself a job as a teacher at the prestigious Dalton School in Manhattan.

Jeffrey Epstein was hired to teach at Dalton in 1974 by Donald Barr who is the father of William "Bill" Barr. Barr began working for the Central Intelligence Agency

(CIA) right after high school. He also worked in Ronald Reagan's White House and held numerous posts within the Department of Justice. Under his advice, President George H. W. Bush pardoned six officials involved in the Iran-Contra affair. This prompted Independent Counsel Lawrence E. Walsh to state that "The Iran-Contra cover-up, which has continued for more than six years, has now been complete." Walsh noted that in issuing the pardons Bush appears to have been preempting being implicated himself in the crimes of Iran-Contra by evidence that was to come to light during the Weinberger trial, and noted that there was a pattern of deception and obstruction by Bush, Weinberger and other senior Reagan administration officials.

Donald Barr's science fiction book *Space Relations* reads like a roadmap for Jeffrey Epstein's criminal life. However, when one delves somewhat into his parents, their lives and their connections to the CIA's MK-Ultra program, the two don't seem like coincidences. This author believes they are part of the same CIA intelligence subset to whom Barr and Epstein both belonged.

Donald Barr was born on August 7, 1921 in New York City. His parents were Simon Pelham Barr and Estelle de Young Barr. In the 1930 census, when Donald was 8 and his sister Margaret 11, they lived at 450 Riverside Drive in the Morningside Heights neighborhood of Manhattan. The apartment building is walking distance to Columbia University and is, in fact, still owned by the college. Columbia University has been facilitating CIA research since the 1950s. Allen Dulles' father-in-law, Professor A. Todd, taught at the school and is believed to have been one of Simon Pelham Barr's professors. His daughter, Clever Todd, who was Dulles wife was the same age as Estelle de Young – both being born in 1893.

Estelle de Young Barr was a psychology major and co-authored *Race Differences in Mental and Physical Traits* published in 1934. She wrote another paper, *A Psychological Analysis of Fashion Motivation* published in the same year which was widely cited for decades afterwards. Estelle worked in eugenics and participated in unwilling group psychological experiments before and after World War II. Everything appears to connect her to working with U.S. intelligence. Furthermore, the CIA has used culture to guide the populace for decades.

The Barr's family connection to Allen Dulles is fascinating. Dulles has been described as a psychopath who allegedly ordered the assassination of President John F. Kennedy.

Dulles was born in 1893 and was a diplomat, a lawyer, a banker, and the longest serving (1953-1961)

Director of the Central Intelligence Agency. Prior to the CIA, he was part of the OSS. He entered diplomatic service in 1916 and married Clover Todd in 1920. His sister Eleanor claimed that Dulles had at least a hundred extramarital affairs. He worked with his brother, John Foster Dulles, at the law firm Sullivan and Cromwell. In 1927 he became a director of the Council on Foreign Relations. It should be noted that Jeffrey Epstein was a member of the Council on Foreign Relations from 1995 until 2009.

In 1954 Isser Harel, Director of Mossad met with Dulles and presented him with an engraved dagger. *'The Guardian of Israel Neither Slumbers or Sleeps.'* He responded with these words: "You can count on me to stay awake with you" thereby cementing the partnership between Mossad and the CIA.

Barr, the headmaster at Dalton, is known within the ranks of the CIA as an "Old Boy". This was the affectionate term for the old-timers who served in the wartime Office of Strategic Services, the forerunner of the CIA. "Old Boys" like Tracy Barnes, Richard Bissell, Frank Wisner, Bronson Tweedy and John Bross ran the agency as if it were a secret society at Yale. They would bring in new recruits from people they knew or met. While the CIA recruited at universities and on campuses of Ivy League schools since the mid-1950s, the practice did not become widespread until the mid-1980s when they began to lose good candidates to Wall Street.

Barr had the educational requirements that made him an ideal candidate for the OSS. He attended Columbia University in New York, as had his parents before him. He majored in mathematics and anthropology, graduating in 1941 in the middle of World War II. He joined the Army teaching math to anti-aircraft gunnery students at an Army camp in Hulen, Texas. In 1945 he became part of the OSS and spent time in Germany investigating industrialists and SS men who'd fled to South America.

Another intelligence connection is William Colby who attended Columbia University at the same time as Barr, and who also served in the OSS at the same time. In 1989 Craig Spence, a spy with an underage blackmail "male prostitution" ring catering to power brokers made the news. Spence held sex parties for key officials of the Reagan and Bush administrations, movie stars, and top military officials. He bugged the gatherings to compromise his guests providing cocaine and boys as young as eleven years old. Among the guests named by *The Washington Times* were journalists Eric Sevareid, Ted Koeppel and William Safire; former CIA Director William Casey; the late John Mitchell who had been Attorney General for Richard Nixon.

Returning to Columbia after the war, Donald resumed his studies, completing his course requirements for a PhD while teaching courses with field work in sociology and political science at Columbia's School of Engineering. During this period, he developed the Science Honors Program which got the attention and support of the National Science Foundation. The Foundation was set up, in part, by the CIA, and signed into law by President Harry S. Truman in 1950. The initial members were all hand-picked by Truman. It is from this perch that that Donald Barr makes his debut at the Dalton school as head master in 1964.

At the age of 21 Jeffrey Epstein began to teach. He was just a couple of years older than his students and he lacked a college degree. In a prep school where parents paid a premium to ensure their offspring received a good education, this was a no-no.

What some of his former students remember about him is interesting: he dressed outrageously. For example, Epstein thought nothing of wearing his shirts open exposing his chest hair and a gold chain he wore around his neck. Other teachers wore crisp white shirts. Furthermore, the students recall him wandering the school halls wearing a long, flamboyant fur coat that seemed more suitable to 1970s Harlem than to 1970s Upper East Side.

A former Dalton student described him as "someone who seemed like he had just walked off the movie *Saturday Night Fever* and was a bit smarmy".

Other students remember him being overly attentive to the girls. A few of them became concerned about a close relationship he developed with a female student who was in the 11th grade. Jon Barnes, who had Epstein as his teacher, also made this claim on Twitter. The girl is described as "the daughter of a very wealthy and powerful Wall Street titan". While it remains unconfirmed, my suspicion is this was Alan "Ace" Greenberg's daughter, Lynne. One of the students became concerned enough to raise the issue with a school administrator.

Epstein was fired at the end of the school year in June 1976 for poor performance.

It was the best thing that could happen to him.

Alan "Ace" Greenberg of Bear Stearns hired him. Jeffrey Epstein still took a train into Manhattan from Brooklyn and was considered by locals who partied to be part of the dreaded bridge and tunnel crowd. But he didn't care if he couldn't get into the hot night spots, he was now in the big leagues and dating the boss's daughter.

When he met Ghislaine Maxwell, the Oxford educated daughter of Robert Maxwell, she was a few weeks shy of her 30th birthday and was too old for him.

Ghislaine Maxwell told her friends she wanted to marry Jeffrey Epstein. To the world they put on a seemingly respectable front. She gave him the patina of glamour and he allowed her to live beyond the restriction of her £80,000-a-year trust fund.

Both felt invincible in January of 1992. Neither one had any inkling that one day their names would be emblazoned on the cover of newspapers across the world as having run an underage sex trafficking and blackmail ring.

A scheme that would implicate some of the most powerful men in the world. Former United States Presidents like Bill Clinton and Donald Trump; as well Prince Andrew, the Duke of York and the favorite son of Queen Elizabeth.

TWENTY-TWO

Scott Borgerson

At six-foot-four Scott Borgerson is an imposing figure. He's also been married to alleged child trafficker Ghislaine Maxwell for some time. If we know anything about Ghislaine, it's that she gravitates towards men who resemble her father. In temperament.

Ill-tempered men with a sadistic streak are the sort of guys she goes for. That she stood by and enabled Jeffrey Epstein for years says it better than any words I can string together. And, it's quite possible the 6'4, dark haired Borgerson might be able fill the giant-sized shoes of her late father, Robert Maxwell.

Maxwell, dubbed *The Bouncing Czech*, was known as much for his jet-black hair and imposing height of 6'3 as he was for his wild mood swings. One minute he could be charming and the next lethal. Some who knew him surmised he might have been bi-polar and claim he definitely had psychotic tendencies.

Scott Borgerson, 43, was the CEO of CargoMetrics – a shipping data company he founded in 2010 until a couple of months ago when he abruptly resigned. On October 2, 2020 Tradewinds broke the story that he stepped down as CEO of his company due to "intense media interest" surrounding his "rumored links with Jeffrey Epstein associate Ghislaine Maxwell".

He has a net worth of approximately $100 million and will be putting up $25 million of a proposed $30 million bond to get Ghislaine Maxwell out of jail and home in time for Christmas (which, by the way is her 59th birthday). Her siblings will be contributing the additional $5 million. A second bail hearing is anticipated to be scheduled and heard on December 21, 2020.

I do not know Scott Borgerson and I do not know if he has the same psychotic tendencies as Robert Maxwell or Jeffrey Epstein, but I do know he frequently told people, including his neighbors, that he aspired to become President of the United States. Having married Ghislaine Maxwell, he can probably scratch this off his wish-list.

Further, the *Daily Mail* reported that when Scott Borgerson's marriage to his first wife Rebecca ended in 2014, divorce records included accusations of him being "physically violent, abuse. 'extremely controlling' and having an alcohol problem". In May 2001 he allegedly threatened Rebecca, saying: 'Don't make me beat you in front of the children.'

The way Borgerson broke the news to his wife that their marriage was over was to send her a video of himself and Ghislaine hugging and kissing. This is dark and more than hints at sadism. It's also the sort of behavior Maxwell knows and loves. What a man.

While he'd told Rebecca he would be in London on business – when she received the video and watched it, along with her two young children, she realized he was actually in Miami with Ghislaine.

Things rapidly deteriorated because on June 15, 2014 Borgerson physically attacked her and was charged with assault and domestic battery (according to court documents).

Some of Ghislaine's victims allege she gets a "thrill" to know she's caused someone else pain. The thought of Scott's wife receiving the video of them smooching like teenagers must have made Ghislaine giddy.

The duo, according to a reliable source, were married abroad.

It wasn't until Maxwell was arrested and had a bail hearing on July 14, 2020 that the world learned she had acquired a "husband".

I live tweeted the court proceedings that day. And, oddly, when US prosecutor Alison Moe claimed Maxwell was married and had a husband whose identity she refused to reveal there was sudden static on the line. It was almost like we'd heard something we weren't supposed to hear. Many of us listening in on the conference call weren't sure what was said exactly. I thought I'd misheard and didn't tweet it out until later.

However, it was confirmed. Ghislaine Maxwell had a husband and no one knew his name. Not even the court. The news practically melted the twittersphere. Who? Who? Who? Guesses ranged from the now deceased Jeffrey Epstein to Prince Andrew. Wrong. Wrong. Wrong.

I immediately recalled she'd gone house hunting with an assumed identity and a "husband" named Scott in tow. So, I tweeted the following:

"The real estate agent who was interrogated by the FBI said the couple who purchased the home identified themselves as Scott and Jen Marshall. Both had British accents. Scott Marshall had explained to her he was retired from the British military and was currently working on a book. Jen described herself as a journalist. The older couple explained they wanted to purchase the property quickly through a "wire and were setting up an LLC". They seemed to her like a "nice couple". It was only after the sale that the real estate agent, having seen a photograph of Ghislaine Maxwell, realized that "Jen" was in fact Ghislaine.'"

Through property records I was able to find that Scott Borgerson, Christine Maxwell (Ghislaine's sister) and Jeffrey W. Roberts were the sole trustees of company named *Angara* that owns a property located at 27 Chestnut Street, Unit 3A, Boston, Massachusetts. As it turns out the condo is Scott's second home to be close to his office in Boston. On September 10, 2018 Christine Maxwell and Jeffrey W. Roberts delegated their powers to Borgerson—

who is now the sole owner. Roberts is also the attorney for Granite Reality LLC (the company used to purchase the ultra-secluded home, Tuckedaway, in New Hampshire where Ghislaine was hiding when she was arrested by the FBI). The same Boston attorney, Jeffrey W. Robert, is also the registered agent of another company associated with Borgerson named *Hopely Yealton.*

Greg Olear, who publishes a wonderful newsletter, *Prevail,* wrote a detailed article after my tweet. It's a deep dive on Scott Borgerson titled, *Ship Shape: Who is Scott Borgerson and What Does Ghislaine Maxwell See in Him?*

It should be noted that Christine Maxwell is the co-founder (with her twin sister Isabel) of Chiliad. Chiliad is a software used by the FBI to store data. It's also used for surveillance by the NSA via their Hewlett Packard servers post 9/11.

One might ask what does Scott Borgerson see in a woman who has been accused of raping children? Perhaps he sees the same thing Jeffrey Epstein saw: a long list of contacts with the wealthiest and most powerful people in the world. Contacts that have allegedly been compromised and would "owe" her something.

It seems clear Ghislaine Maxwell did not leave the United States for safer shores because of her husband: Scott Borgerson. It is now up to him to repay the favor. He is doing so now at the cost of his business, his children and $25 million. The money, however, belonged to Maxwell who transferred it to him while fending off lawsuits.

By the time of Ghislaine's trial which began on November 29, 2021 Scott Borgerson was dating a woman named Kris McGinn. McGinn is described by the New York Post as a "local writer, mother of two high school children and yoga enthusiast who has an ass that could crack open a walnut".

Borgerson was a no show in court for his wife, Ghislaine Maxwell.

TWENTY-THREE

Ghislaine Maxwell's Arrest

———————

After the death of Jeffrey Epstein on August 10, 2019 Ghislaine Maxwell simply vanished. Headlines across the world with the words: *Where in the World is Ghislaine Maxwell* were commonplace. Many concluded she was hiding in France, others suggested England, while some claimed she was surely being hidden by the Mossad in Israel.

As it turned out Ghislaine Maxwell was living in a sleepy town named Bradford in New Hampshire – only a few hours north of New York City. New Hampshire is the largest State in New England. It is tucked between Massachusetts to the south and Vermont to the West. It is the fifth smallest state covering 300 square miles with a population of under 1.3 million.

On July 2, 2020 sixty FBI agents, with local police officers, showed up on the 156-acre estate belonging to an anonymized company called 'Granite Reality, LLC'. The $1 million home at 338 East Washington Road was purchased on December 3, 2019 in an all-cash transaction. Two helicopters circled the skies since 4:20am on that fateful Tuesday morning. The FBI wanted to make sure they would be able to track Maxwell's movements in the event she left the house before the agents arrived.

Four hours later, at approximately 8:30am, a combination of local police and FBI agents made their way through the long driveway of the estate appropriately named 'Tuckedaway'. They were able to determine the dark-haired woman they spotted through the glass window was Ghislaine Maxwell. One of them knocked loudly on the huge door and shouted "FBI!"

Ghislaine Maxwell was startled. She immediately got up off the sofa and ran into one of the bedrooms locking the door behind her. Some accounts claim she hid under the bed.

The agents then rammed through the front door of the opulent home. Windows and glass doors shattered sending shards of glass in every direction. Her cat ran off into the huge expanse of land surrounding the property. Dozens of local and federal agents marched inside. They were able to take Maxwell into custody. Not once did she believe this would ever happen to her although there are hints that she was afraid of this in emails between herself and Jeffrey Epstein years earlier.

Maxwell has a pilot's license as well as a submarine license, and she's the daughter of Robert Maxwell, Mossad "superspy," as identified by authors Gordon Thomas and Martin Dillon. Given Robert Maxwell's history and Ghislaine's involvement in Jeffrey Epstein's life, one would almost expect her to pull off a movie-worthy martial arts move – such as leaping into the air as she bounced off the ceiling and walls, then slithering away as a sneering wicked cartoon figure. Instead, the 58-year-old Ghislaine Maxwell did her best to fight back tears as she was escorted off to Merrimack Country Jail. One week later she was transported to the Metropolitan Detention Center in Brooklyn, New York where human traffickers Keith Raniere and Clare Bronfman of the NXIVM cult were being held.

Ghislaine Maxwell's cellphone, which agents retrieved, had been covered in tin foil. It was said by law enforcement officials to be an attempt at evading detection. She had also recently changed her email address and registered a new phone under the name "G Max". One of the FBI agents bragged that arresting her was "sweeter than that of notorious U.S. gangster James 'Whitey' Bulger".

The female real estate agent who sold the house to Ghislaine Maxwell was interrogated by the FBI. She explained to them that she'd sold to a couple who identified themselves as Scott and Jen Marshall. Both had British accents. Scott Marshall explained he was retired from the British military and was currently working on a book. Jen told her she was a journalist. They expressed a desire to purchase the property quickly through a "wire and were setting up an LLC". It was only after the sale that the real estate agent, having seen a photograph of Ghislaine Maxwell, realized "Jen" was Ghislaine Maxwell.

It should be noted that In Maxwell's younger days she would have been familiar with her father's Mossad handler: Rafi Eitan.

Eitan was a master of disguise. As an Israeli superspy he was accustomed to moving unobtrusively in the shadowy world of espionage. In 1960 Eitan and his team of agents dressed up as El Al stewards when he captured the Nazi war criminal Adolph Eichmann and brought him back to Israel to stand trial. In 1983 Eitan simply changed his name and identified himself as Dr. Benn Orr when he purchased a plane ticket on December 19, 1982 and flew to the United States. He preferred flying during the beginning of a holiday season as the airport was especially crowded and the officials were too busy to ask many questions. Upon arriving at Kennedy Airport Eitan presented his Israeli passport which identified him as Dr. Benjamin Orr, assistant public prosecutor in the Ministry of Justice in Tel Aviv, Israel. He preferred to lie "about the truth". There was a real Dr. Orr. He had worked for the Justice Department. However, the real Dr. Orr was retired and the passport used by Eitan was a forgery. It is this writer's opinion that this is the way Ghislaine Maxwell lied. She used minor details like names and occupations to keep her pretense for the real estate agent real enough.

Scott Borgerson had been identified as the man Maxwell was living with in his oceanfront property in Manchester by the Sea, near Boston in the summer of 2019. Borgerson is said to have left his wife, Rebecca, in order to be with Ghislaine. This is where Ghislaine got the name "Scott" from without a doubt. Her father, Robert Maxwell, was a publisher, and labeling herself a "journalist" is almost too easy to connect. The couple was said to have British accents and so it is highly probable the fake "Scott" was one of her brothers. Kevin or Ian – who are linked with the house and the LLC that was being used to pay her expenses.

Upon her arrest it was discovered she had former British security guards providing round the clock protection. Papers filed for the case state that one of the guards informed investigators it had been one of her brothers who hired them to guard her in rotation. They ran errands for her. One was even trusted with a credit card in the name of the same limited liability corporation that had purchased the house. He would go and buy supplies for her so that she wouldn't have to venture out.

One of Maxwell's friends told *The Sun* that, "Ghislaine has been constantly on the move throughout the last year. She would stay in properties for a few days or a week." The source added, "Security guards were by her side due to death threats".

In a public announcement, the Southern District of New York (SDNY), stated Ghislaine Maxwell had assisted Jeffrey Epstein in his abuse of minor girls. One of the prosecutors said, "Between 1994 and 1997

Maxwell played a critical role in helping Epstein to befriend and groom minors for abuse."

Additionally, prosecutors added "the couple would pick out girls, asking them about their lives and pretending to take an interest in them, taking them to the movies and shopping trips. All of which then turned into sexual abuse." What is startling to victims and to those who have followed this case is that she was not charged with abusing the very minors she is alleged to have "befriended, groomed and transported". Furthermore, the dates represent only three years in a trafficking scheme Maxwell was alleged to have participated in for over 15 years. Add to this the big names in the case such as Bill Clinton and Prince Andrew fall outside of the three-year period. And, not least of all, the first person to have reported Ghislaine Maxwell, along with Jeffrey Epstein and many other high-profile names to the FBI in 1995, sexual abuse victim Maria Farmer, is mysteriously missing from the list of charges. In Maria's case she reported much more than sexual assault – she reported that she was almost murdered while on the property of Jeffrey Epstein's patron, the CEO and owner of L Brands & Victoria's Secret, Leslie Wexner.

According to her accusers, Ghislaine Maxwell was Jeffrey Epstein's protector and procurer. His "soul mate and mirror image". In an interview Epstein gave to *Vanity Fair* in 2003 he describes Maxwell, 41 at the time, as his "best friend". He claimed she is not on his payroll, but "seems to organize much of his life". Janusz Banasiak, a former house manager for Jeffrey Epstein, said in court records, "They were like partners in business."

Some of the victims claim they never saw them holding hands like a normal couple or even sleeping in the same bed.

Until the day of Ghislaine Maxwell's bail hearing on July 14, 2020 she had not been seen by the public. That is with the exception of a bizarre photo op on August 12, 2019 - just two days after Jeffrey Epstein's death which is an important detail that should not be overlooked.

On August 15, 2019 *The New York Post* ran a story named, *Jeffrey Epstein's gal pal Ghislaine Maxwell spotted at In-N-Out Burger in first photos since his death*. It states:

"Jeffrey Epstein's former gal pal Ghislaine Maxwell isn't holed up in her British manor or summering on the Massachusetts coast.

The Post found the socialite hiding in plain sight in the least likely place imaginable — a fast-food joint in Los Angeles.

Maxwell, 57, the alleged madam to the multimillionaire pedophile, was scarfing down a burger, fries and shake al fresco at an In-N-Out Burger on Monday while reading 'The Book of Honor: The Secret Lives and Deaths of Secret CIA Operatives,' a nonfiction best-seller by journalist Ted Gup.

Sitting alone with a pet pooch, she was surprised to have been found and told an onlooker, 'Well, I guess this is the last time I'll be eating here!'"

The photos were immediately debunked as a staged ploy by Ghislaine Maxwell and one of her attorneys, Leah Saffian. The dog belonged to Saffian and was found on her Instagram. The photos' metadata were linked to a media company owned by Saffian and found to have been taken by a professional photographer. The camera was deemed to have a sophisticated lens instead of that of a smartphone as the Post had suggested. Which then begs the question, how is the New York Post involved in the on-going cover-up of the crimes of Jeffrey Epstein and his co-conspirators? We should perhaps extend that to other newspapers that have covered this story such as *The Sun*. After all Rupert Murdoch, who owns *The Sun* has been a friend to Ghislaine Maxwell for decades. Murdoch was also listed in Jeffrey Epstein's infamous black book.

In the photos staged by Ghislaine and her friend Leah Saffian she appeared different. Gone are the society designer label clothes and the Manolo Blahnik pumps. There is even a hole in the pair of sneakers Ghislaine wears for the mysterious photo op. In lieu of a perfectly made-up face are stark black framed glasses. The artifice is gone. She is bare to be seen and it is intentional.

Not least of all is that the woman who claimed "never to eat" for fear of gaining weight is at a fast-food burger joint sitting out in the open on the sidewalk. The internet blew up trying to decode the message she was clearly trying to send. In this writer's opinion her message was confirmation that Jeffrey Epstein had indeed been a spy and if she were not to be left alone, she would reveal further incriminating information on the "lives of operatives".

Some speculate the 'Inn-N-Out' Burger photos in Los Angeles were meant as a distraction after various media reports surfaced days earlier that she was living in a secluded Massachusetts mansion with her new beau, Scott Borgerson.

Borgerson is a member of the Council of Foreign Relations and the founder and CEO of CargoMetrics Technologies. The company analyzes data on global shipping according to his bio on *LinkedIn*. On October

2, 2020 it was reported that Borgerson had resigned from the company he founded in 2010 because of the "intense media interest surrounding his rumored links with Jeffrey Epstein associate Ghislaine Maxwell".

On July 14, 2020 when Ghislaine Maxwell appeared at her bail hearing, she looked different to many. Some people speculated she'd had cosmetic surgery. A drawing emerged showing her with her hair pulled away from her face and in a bun. She was said to be 20 or 30 lbs heavier. For a woman who was vain about her appearance and who constantly worked out, many found this odd.

Equally extreme and unusual was her request, via her attorneys, that she be allowed to live in a luxury Manhattan hotel on bail while awaiting her trial. In barely heard whispers the prosecutors revealed Ghislaine Maxwell was married. Because of the Covid pandemic the hearing was on a live audio feed for up to 1,000 members of the press and the public who wanted to hear it – limited to 500 people – and then because of the demand it was expanded to 1,000. I was one of those who heard the hearing and live-tweeted the proceeding. When it was revealed that Ghislaine was married the audio was so poor few people heard it. The prosecution revealed Ghislaine's new status with the following statement:

"In addition to failing to describe in any way the absence of proposed co-signers of a bond, the defendant also makes no mention whatsoever about the financial circumstances or assets of her spouse whose identity she declined to provide to Pretrial Services," Assistant US Attorney Alison Moe told Manhattan federal Judge Alison Nathan during the video conference.

Had Ghislaine Maxwell been preparing to run? *'Very likely'* was the chatter on social media. Was she going to run alone? No. Maxwell had acquired a husband.

During the hearing there was another bombshell, her attorneys claimed the house in New Hampshire did not belong to her. They said the house was only on loan to her and that she had obtained "permission to live there". They offered Maxwell's home in London as part of the bail – which is ludicrous because property in another country cannot be used as leverage. Ghislaine seemed uncooperative even in her request for bail. Her attorneys offered a $5 million bond secured by an unnamed group of what they described as "six financially responsible people, all of whom have strong ties to Ms. Maxwell."

In arguments for detention the Assistant U.S. Attorney Alison Moe described Maxwell as "a woman of mystery but seemingly inexhaustible means, international connections, multiple foreign bank accounts, and three passports." She argued that her risk of flight is extreme. Maxwell's ability to hide during the year that Epstein was indicted was also brought up as one of the reasons to deny her request.

Judge Alison Nathan deemed Maxwell a flight risk and ordered her to be detained until her trial on July 12, 2021.

Ghislaine Maxwell lost what little composure she managed to summon up and dried a tear drop from her eye.

EPILOGUE

Victoria's Secret

————————

At 5'10' with long blonde hair and a perfect face the teenager stood out from her classmates at the local high school she attended. The stores in her neighborhood—one of eight districts in Vlaardingen—an old harbor town in the province of South

Holland, the Netherlands all carried the glossy fashion magazines.

The area is a beacon for factories and ship repair businesses. On the Vulcaanhaven—the largest privately owned artificial harbor in the world—is the factory for Faberge cosmetics. Perhaps this is why fashion magazines regularly line the racks of the supermarkets and newspaper stands throughout the city.

Karen Mulder had been mesmerized by these images on the pages of the glossy magazines. She fantasized about what it would be like to be one of the beautiful models who looked as if they didn't have a care in the world and who wore the most amazing designer clothes.

In 1985 her parents took her and her younger sister, Saskia, on a camping trip in the south of France. This is where she first saw the ad for Elite Model Management's *Look of the Year* contest. Her eyes fixated on it and for several minutes she allowed herself to daydream. But reality got the better of her. They wouldn't want a teenager wearing braces, she silently scolded herself, settling back into reality.

One of her friends, however, decided to send photos of the statuesque teen to *Elite* without her knowledge. To her astonishment she won the preliminary contest which was held in Amsterdam. Things moved quickly and she ascended up to the finals where she won second place. From here Karen was signed by the agency and before she knew what was happening she was no longer in high school but on the runways.

Elite Model Management was founded in 1972 in Paris, France by John Casablancas.

He is remembered as a man with a sexual preference for teenage girls. When Casablancas was 41, he began having a sexual relationship with Stephanie Seymour—who was 15 years old. Seymour met the modeling world mogul at one of his many modeling competitions. He explained his views on Seymour in an interview,

"[Seymour] is a girl of extremes...and the way she developed—there's a quality about her that is this incredible sensuality that a woman-child has, a true woman-child...her voice is a child's, her attitudes, the way she holds her feet and her hands are those of a child, at the same time with an incredibly sensuality to it. And that mixture was and is so explosive...This was something like a forbidden fruit for both of us".

Gerard Marie became the President of *Elite* and has been accused by many models, including Carré Otis, of rape. Otis began working for *Elite* when she was 17 and as a struggling young model was sleeping in Gerard Marie's home where she was still required to pay rent. After finding Marie's cocaine stash in the bathroom she says the two developed an "age-inappropriate" bond over snorting the class-A drug. He told the impressionable teenager the drug was "the secret to model weight management."

Adnan Khashoggi is one of many men to whom the models were allegedly "pimped out". One of *Elite's* models said in an interview that Khashoggi routinely browsed through photo portfolios of the young aspiring models. After his review his assistant would ask him who he would like. It was for Khashoggi, and men like him, similar to ordering a side of fries with one's lunch. A meet-up fee of $35,000 to $50,000 would be arranged with the agency.

The seedy side of the modeling world was investigated by *60 Minutes* in 1988 where Jean-Luc Brunel—a friend of Ghislaine Maxwell's—was alleged by several young models aged between 15 and 18 of sexual harassment and rape. The same allegations had been made for over three decades. However, no criminal investigation was launched.

Epstein gave Brunel a $1 million line of credit to provide him with girls. Virginia Giuffre former "sex-slave" of Epstein and Maxwell claimed in a deposition that the modeling agency was really a front for trafficking.

The underbelly of this world—where the agencies owned not only your face but your body to do with what they wanted—was not known to Karen Mulder when she embarked on her modeling career. Before she was 17 she was modeling for fashion icons like Valentino, Yves Saint Laurent, Versace and Giorgio Armani. In a *New York Times* article entitled *'Fashion: Striking Poses'* Ellen Harth, head of Elite Runway Inc., said of models like Naomi Campbell, Claudia Schiffer and Karen Mulder, "They are sensual, not sexy."

She goes on to describe Karen Mulder as a rare commodity, a radiant blonde with undertones of sultriness and adds,

"Mulder is that rare commodity, a mannequin who can turn a rigorously plain dress into one as alluring as a satin negligee. 'She could sell a paper bag,' says Harth, her agent. And indeed, at Calvin Klein's presentation Mulder's voluptuous outline and undulating walk transformed an understated gray tunic into a seductive showpiece."

The worlds of Karen Mulder, Ghislaine Maxwell, Jeffrey Epstein had already collided when she signed her first modeling contract. In the beginning she went along with the unsettling string of events. She thought it was part of the world of grown-ups. The incredibly long hours, the drugs to keep her working, and the endless men whose hands feverishly reached up between her thighs.

On January 5, 1992 just two weeks after the tribute for her father at *The Plaza Hotel* Ghislaine Maxwell and Jeffrey Epstein flew to Paris for fashion week. Epstein was close with Leslie Wexner of Victoria's Secret and the two shared mutual friends.

Leslie Wexner was a billionaire and a Zionist. Wexner like her father Robert Maxwell shared the same goals for Israel. In July of 1991 he had signed Power of Attorney over to Epstein.

Jeffrey Epstein had been working with him since 1985 even though he also worked with Steven Hoffenberg. Hoffenberg, however, had recently come under scrutiny by the Securities and Exchange Commission (SEC) for trading stock while in possession of nonpublic information as well as for the Ponzi scheme they ran out of their offices at the Villard Houses. Epstein reassured Ghislaine that nothing was going to happen to him.

Arriving at the Valentino Haute Couture fashion show they moved in harmony with the crowd and took their seats, champagne flutes in hand, and folding their coats on their laps while the loud music filled the room. Two photographers flitted about the room snapping photos of anyone who looked famous. Almost everyone was in one way or another. This was a by-invitation only event. When one of them approached the couple, Epstein instinctively faced forward closing his eyes. Ghislaine, more accustomed to the demands of the press, looked straight into the camera with a half-hearted Mona Lisa smile.

Soon the lights dim and the models began to walk the runway. Ghislaine elbows Jeffrey when she sees their friend Naomi Campbell step onto the runway. Then Karen Mulder takes the stage. She's radiant in a white sleeveless sheath dress paired off with white fishnet stockings.

After this event Mulder is offered a contract with Wexner's Victoria's Secret which she accepts. (I should preface this by saying that one of my sources told me she was there at the afterparty for this fashion show. She alleges Mulder was forced into having sex with Epstein. That, in fact, she too was expected to have sex with Epstein. I add this only as an anecdote and not as a fact as I have no way of checking whether or not it is true. Based on what we know about this case—it seems true. However, I wish to respect the boundaries of journalism. I only have one source. A terrified source. A source that even today, 30 years later, is too afraid to step forward).

By the time Karen Mulder joins Victoria's Secret their catalog has been sent out from the company's corporate headquarters in Columbus, Ohio for decades. Their list includes some of the wealthiest and most powerful men in the world. The men may not like the third-rate fabric of the skimpy lingerie—but that is not what they're looking at as they thumb through each issue. Few of them discard it keeping it instead with their stash of Playboy magazines.

In 2001 Karen appears on a French television show and tells a horrified host that she has been raped by top executives at *Elite* as well as being given as a gift to Prince Albert of Monaco. She alleges she has been coerced into having sex to garner better contracts, that *Elite* had used her and other models as sex slaves in a ring that extended through the top echelons of French society, implicating politicians, members of the police, and other top officials. She also claims that her own father had raped her. She complains her bosses got her addicted to cocaine and heroin.

Mulder adds, "They tried to turn me into a prostitute because they thought it would be so easy."

The show never aired and the master tape of the interview was destroyed.

Once back in her apartment in Paris, her sister arrives, and against her will Karen is placed in the psychiatric unit of Montsouris Hospital located in the

14th arrondissement of Paris. Here she is heavily sedated for five months and treated for depression and anxiety. Gerald Marie, the head of *Elite Paris* and one of the men Mulder had accused of raping her, paid her bill.

After her release Karen was found unresponsive on the floor of her apartment. Newspapers reported that she was rushed to the hospital by her former fiancé, Jean Yves Le Fur. On December 11, 2002 *Page Six* wrote:

"Troubled Dutch supermodel Karen Mulder is in a coma after she overdosed on sleeping pills Monday in an apparent attempt to take her own life. The blonde beauty, who drew snickers last year when she claimed to have been raped by everybody from Prince Albert of Monaco to members of her own entourage, was rushed to the American Hospital in Neuilly after her former fiancé, Jean Yves Le Fur, found her passed out on the floor of her Paris apartment. Doctors are still trying to revive her. Mulder's parents flew from the Netherlands to be by her side. Elite models president Gerald Marie, an old friend of Mulder who paid her bills when she was committed to the Montsouris Clinic after her meltdown last year, was shocked. 'It's very sad,' he told PAGE SIX's Jared Paul Stern. 'She had everything. I don't know how she lost it all. Her parents must be freaking out again. It's really a pity. I'm trying to find out what I can do.' Mulder seemed on the road to recovery last

summer when she embarked on a singing career, hitting the French charts with a Gloria Gaynor cover."

The people in her circle state it was her neighbors who found her. In Karen's personal notes she wrote, "Jean-Yves Le Fur is never short of publicity."

Her father, Ben, told the press Karen is full of "mad ideas". This story is echoed by mainstream media. Soon the world believes Karen Mulder is unhinged. That she is crazy.

Once recovered she is made to make a public apology to Prince Albert of Monaco.

Jean-Yves Le Fur is among the many names in Jeffrey Epstein's black book.

～

To present day only three people have been arrested in relation to the sex trafficking ring that spans several continents and appears to include thousands of people.

On July 6, 2019 Jeffrey Epstein is arrested for sex trafficking crimes against minors. Less than six weeks later on August 10, 1991 he is found unresponsive in his cell. His death is declared a suicide by hanging.

On May 3, 2021 it was announced that July trial against Ghislaine Maxwell was postponed to the fall.

On December 17, 2020 Jean-Luc Brunel was arrested at Charles de Gaulle Airport and was taken into custody on counts of rape and sexual assault. Virginia Giuffre contacted the French authorities and told them about having been forced by Jeffrey Epstein and Ghislaine Maxwell to have sex with the modeling agent who she said played "a major role" in their sex trafficking ring.

On June 16, 2021 Giuffre appeared in a Paris courtroom to testify against Jean-Luc Brunel. Giuffre alleges she was forced to have sex with Prince Andrew and other power men, including Jean-Luc Brunel and Leslie Wexner. Brunel had been considered "untouchable" by the police who nicknamed him 'The Ghost'.

Virginia Giuffre told the court she was raped by Brunel in the early 2000s, including in 2001. She said the rapes had taken place mainly in Jeffrey Epstein's homes and his private island of Little Saint James – which had been dubbed 'Orgy Island'.

In Virginia Giuffre's sworn testimony she alleges Jean-Luc Brunel and Prince Andrew, the Duke of York, among other men raped her at Epstein's private island.

EXHIBIT A

Virginia Giuffre's Deposition, Excerpt

———————

The following are excerpts from Virginia Roberts Giuffre deposition taken for the defamation lawsuit against Ghislaine Maxwell on May 3, 2016. I included these here as it fills in the role Virginia played in the lives of Jeffrey Epstein and Ghislaine Maxwell. It explains in her own words who they "lent her out to" during the time she was their alleged sex slave.

Virginia Giuffre, Deposition

Q. Is it your contention that Ghislaine Maxwell sexually trafficked you to famous people?

A. If you have a document in front of you that you could show me so I could see what you're talking about, yes.

Q. I'm asking you, is it your contention that Ghislaine Maxwell sexually trafficked you to famous people?

A. Could you be more specific, like are we talking about rock stars or royalty or –

Q. Politically connected and financially powerful people.

A. Yes.

Q. Okay. To whom did Ghislaine Maxwell sexually traffic you?

A. You have to understand that Jeffrey and Ghislaine are joined hip by hip, okay? So, they both trafficked me. Ghislaine brought me in for the purpose of being trafficked. Jeffrey was just as a part of it as she was. She was just as a part of it as he was. They trafficked me to many people. And to be honest, there is people I could name and then there's people that are just a blur. There was so much happening.

Q. Okay. Please name a person that Ghislaine Maxwell directed you to go have sex with?

A. Eva and Glenn Dubin.

Q. Okay, who else?

A. As a whole, they both trafficked me to people. It was under both of their direction. So, it's not easy just to say Ghislaine. When I say they, I mean both of them.

Q. Okay. Well, I need you to say a time when Ghislaine Maxwell directed you to go have sex with another person. So, can you please tell me to whom Ghislaine Maxwell asked you to go have sex with another person?

MR. EDWARDS: Object to the form.

Q. (BY MS. MENNINGER) Who else?

A. I'm going to continue to tell you that they both directed me to do it. It was part of my training. They both told me, you've got tickets to go here. This is who you're meeting, and this is what you're doing. So is another one.

Q. Ghislaine Maxwell directed you to go have sex with?

MR. EDWARDS: Object to the form to the extent it mischaracterized her testimony.

A. I'm trying to tell you that they both did, Ghislaine and Jeffrey both directed me. They both paid me and they both directed me.

Q. (BY MS. MENNINGER) All right. When did Ghislaine Maxwell direct you to go have sex with ____?

MR. EDWARDS: Object to the form. Same objection.

A. I don't know the time. I don't -- you know, I could tell you the place. I don't know the time.

Q. (BY MS. MENNINGER) What words did Ghislaine Maxwell use in talking to you and asking you to go have sex with ____ ?

A. We're sending you to a gentleman. We want you to show him a good time. We want you to do exactly what you would do for Jeffrey to him. Keep him happy. I can't remember her exact words, and I'm not going to put words in my mouth to make it sound like what she said. But it was all along those lines.

Q. Those are words that Ghislaine Maxwell used in directing you to go have sex with ____?

MR. EDWARDS: Object to the form. Mischaracterized her testimony.

A. Along those lines, yes.

Q. (BY MS. MENNINGER) Okay. Where were you located when she used those words with you?

A. It could have been Palm Beach. It could have been New York.

Q. You don't recall?

A. I don't recall.

Q. Okay. How old were you when she used those words to you?

MR. EDWARDS: Object to the form. Mischaracterizes her testimony.

A. I don't know. I would think I was 17.

Q. (BY MS. MENNINGER) But you're not sure?

A. Well, it was in the beginning, like after my training. Glenn and Eva Dubin are the two first people I was sent out to.

Q. Okay. Well, I was asking about okay?

A. Right. That's what I'm saying. If you want me to categorically tell you when it happened and why I think I was 17, because those were the two first people I was sent to.

Q. So you don't actually recall the conversation regarding the Dubins? You don't recall where you were, right?

A. I can't picture if it was New -- I know it was either New York or Palm Beach. I don't remember exactly which one.

Q. You don't recall exactly what words were used by Ghislaine Maxwell in speaking to you, correct?

A. I remember the tone that she used, the type of words that she used. I can't word for word replay what she said.

Q. All right. And so, when in time was ___ ?

A. _____ was months, six months, I'm not too sure.

Q. Six months what?

A. Before. I don't know, I think I met Prince Andrew in 2001. And Glenn Dubin and Stephen Kaufmann were, like I said, the first 3 people I was sent out to after my training. So, I don't know. I'm not going to give you an exact time if I don't know it.

Q. I asked you the relative order.

A. And I'm trying to give you it.

Q. And where does Alan Dershowitz fit into that group of people?

A. Same. I can't tell you piece by piece by piece who -- I know Glenn Dubin was first.

Q. Okay.

A. And I know Stephen Kaufmann was one of the first I was sent to. Alan Dershowitz could have been between there. Between, sorry, between Glenn and Stephen. The first time I was with Alan Dershowitz was in New York, so I wasn't actually sent to him. It actually happened at one of Jeffrey's residences.

(Ms. McCawley left the deposition.)

A. So, it's very hard for me to chronologically give you each person individually.

Q. (BY MS. MENNINGER) Okay. Name the other politically connected and financially powerful people that Ghislaine Maxwell told you to go have sex with?

A. Again, I'm going to tell you "they" because that's how it went. They instructed me to go to George Mitchell, Jean-Luc Brunel, Bill Richardson, another prince that I don't know his name. A guy that owns a hotel, a really large hotel chain, I can't remember which hotel it was. Marvin Minsky. There was, you know, another foreign president, I can't remember his name. He was Spanish. There's a whole bunch of them that I just - - it's hard for me to remember all of them. You know, I was told to do something by these people constantly, told to -- my whole life revolved around just pleasing these men and keeping Ghislaine and Jeffrey happy. Their whole entire lives revolved around sex. They call massages sex. They call modeling sex.

ABOUT THE AUTHOR

Kirby Sommers is the author of over a dozen books. She is an investigative journalist an advocate for human rights. She writes the weekly *Epstein Project* newsletter and hosts the *Epstein Project* podcast. Her books include *The Billionaire's Woman: A Memoir, Jeffrey Epstein Predator Spy*, *Jeffrey Epstein, Revealed* (co-authored with Bob Fitrakis),

Bonnie's Clyde: The True Story of Jeffrey Epstein and Ghislaine Maxwell, and several others. For a full list, please visit her website: kirbysommers.com.

Kirby's ability to transcend and help others was featured in a Tedx Talk presented by Justin Constantine titled, *You Are Stronger Than You Think You Are.*

Ms. Sommers lives in New York and is currently writing a sequel to her memoir *The Billionaire's Woman* named *Cinderella Doesn't Live Here Anymore*; as well the sequel to *Ghislaine Maxwell: An Unauthorized Biography* titled *Ghislaine Maxwell, Blackmail.* Both books are scheduled for release in the Summer of 2023.

Ghislaine Maxwell: An Unauthorized Biography

Website: kirbysommers.com

Twitter: @kirbysommers

Kirby Sommers

Printed in Great Britain
by Amazon